PU

Princ
Swap

Don't miss any adventures in

The Princess Swap

Cinderella and the Beast
(or, Beauty and the Glass Slipper)

Snow White and the Dragon
(or, Sleeping Beauty and the Seven Dwarfs)

Cinderella and the Beast

The Princess Swap

Beauty and the Glass Slipper

Kim Bussing

PUFFIN

PUFFIN BOOKS

UK | USA | Canada | Ireland | Australia
India | New Zealand | South Africa

Puffin Books is part of the Penguin Random House group of companies
whose addresses can be found at global.penguinrandomhouse.com.

www.penguin.co.uk
www.puffin.co.uk
www.ladybird.co.uk

Penguin Random House UK

First published in the USA by Random House Children's Books,
a division of Penguin Random House LLC, New York,
and in Great Britain by Puffin Books 2025
001

Printed and bound in Great Britain by Clays Ltd, Elcograf S.p.A.

The authorized representative in the EEA is Penguin Random House Ireland,
Morrison Chambers, 32 Nassau Street, Dublin D02 YH68

A CIP catalogue record for this book is available from the British Library

ISBN: 978-0-241-74534-2

All correspondence to:
Puffin Books
Penguin Random House Children's
One Embassy Gardens, 8 Viaduct Gardens, London SW11 7BW

FSC MIX
Paper | Supporting responsible forestry
FSC® C018179
www.fsc.org

Penguin Random House is committed to a sustainable future for our business, our readers and our planet. This book is made from Forest Stewardship Council® certified paper.

To my mother

For all the nocturnes, lake walks, and
afternoons spent over marionberry biscuits
and coffee that gave me the inspiration and
courage to chase after my Big Dreams

Once upon a time, in a land called Reverie, where magic flowed in the water and the wind, where enchantments were as common as loose coins and curses were, too, where all the stories that you've ever heard were true, there was a very, very bad princess.

She lived in a tall castle the color of the rising sun, in a city on the cliffs above the sea. And if you didn't know any better—and most people didn't—she might look like the good kind of princess. She had beautiful dark hair and beautiful green eyes, but her heart was off-center and warped at the edges.

To be honest, it wasn't really her fault.

Many people from all over Reverie passed through the castle's doors: wicked ex-stepmothers and good witches and mermaids with temporary legs; dwarfs that dwelled in the deep and swans that became girls only in the moonlight. They came to speak to the queen, to negotiate and barter and plead, and the princess watched them from afar, before being dragged off by a nursemaid, or a dancing tutor, or the cook.

She was just as good at fencing and archery as her twin brother, just as quick with numbers and figures as the king's treasurer, and perhaps better than the king at unpuzzling complex negotiations.

But a princess wasn't meant to do anything like that. A princess was meant to sit and be told she was pretty and receive gifts, silver-backed mirrors and jeweled birds and tin forests with tiny tin squirrels that would throw tiny tin acorns at you if you got too close. She wasn't allowed to leave the castle—for her own good, they said. They didn't even call her by name—just *the princess,* like she was a piece of furniture they needed, instead of a girl.

From her bedroom window the princess would see the birds swarm in the sky, the horned and hoofed beasts leap through the briars, the mousing cats curl in patches of sunlight, and would wish and wish and wish to be among them.

But since her wishes weren't being answered, the princess did the next best thing, which was try not to be bored.

She put tar on the palace steps when the ex-stepmothers left so they'd get stuck. She stuffed the good witches into the larder and put frogs in the royal librarian's tea. She pinched and teased and stole, because at least she was doing something.

It was dangerous, living in Reverie, because it meant that a fairy might visit. And fairies were known for their whims and for sometimes being a little too quick to grant wishes.

And when one did visit, when a fairy heard about all the princess's nastiness, that fairy enacted his favorite kind of punishment on the bad princess. He gave her what wishes usually give—exactly what she thought she wanted.

Don't tell anyone you're reading this.

In fact, maybe it's best you don't read this at all.

Because these pages are full of curses and contests, fairies and goblin attacks, betrayal and magical clocks. And in a story filled with so much magic, it's too easy for some of the magic to spill out. To latch on to your wishes and make them come true, too.

Be careful. Or you might find yourself in the wrong story.

1

Ella

IT ISN'T THAT ELLA LIKES SLEEPING IN THE fireplace. And she knows that it only gives her stepsisters, Fiona and Marie—although mostly Fiona—more reasons to pick on her and pull her hair and leave her only charred bits of oats for breakfast, saying if she likes the cinders so much, she might as well eat them.

It's just that when Ella lies at the bottom of the chimney and stares up, she can see the stars, and on each of them she imagines an adventure: that she is a prima donna in Apfel, a queen of thieves, or even a toymaker. And sometimes she imagines for so long that she falls asleep and wakes up to the clink-clunk of her stepmother's tin bell, or Fiona kicking her and calling her "Cinderella."

Except today, Ella isn't in the fireplace. She's in a bed.

A soft bed. Early-morning sunlight scatters over a small, mostly untouched room. The ceiling slopes over her head like the inside of a globe, a few stacks of leather-bound journals totter in the corners, and there's a brassy nautical spyglass on a wobbly desk.

Ella bolts up, shoving a blue quilt off her. A pang shoots through the knee above her glass leg, and confusion shoots through the rest of her.

This isn't right.

This isn't Marie's room, which always has plates etched with the dried remains of chocolate cake, or Fiona's, littered with the odds and ends she demands that her mother buy her from the market.

And this is certainly not her stepmother's room, where everything smells like her cloying perfume and pipe smoke.

If this is one of her stepsisters' jokes—well, then they're a little more clever than Ella gave them credit for. All Ella knows is that she needs to get out of here before Simone realizes she's gone; her stepmother doesn't take kindly to her breakfast being late. Not that Ella cares if Simone gets her toast or not, but she does care about the extra chores that will be forced upon her if Simone gets into one of her moods.

Ella limps over to the window, the knee above her glass leg aching. And she gasps.

Ella's expecting the pink stone buildings of Miravale, one of the five capital cities of Reverie's five kingdoms.

She expects the busy cobblestoned streets, the distant spire of the royal castle. This is—

Sheep.

Green hills tumble past the window, dotted with woolly bodies, a few oak trees.

Ella's not just *not home.* She's very, very far from home.

It seems Simone's toast will be late after all.

And Ella . . . Ella has no idea how she got here. Or who brought her.

Still. Escape first. Worry second.

Ella shoves the window up, the smell of fresh grass and clover riding the summer breeze. But she pauses once more; a little square clock is propped on the windowsill, its sides painted with roses. Ella's fingers twitch. The time is wrong—it can't be *that* late in the morning—but it reminds her of a picture her father showed her once, and she stuffs it into her pocket. With everything that reminds her of her father, she feels an almost irrational desire to hold it close, like a person can be put back together with mementos.

Ella swings her good leg over the windowsill, wincing at the pain in her left knee. Below the knee is a glass leg. She's had it since she was younger, but it's been hurting more and more recently.

Someone coughs.

"What are—who are—why are you—" A man with a whirlwind of white hair splutters in the doorway. His eyes widen as he takes in her half-successful window escape. “There are *stairs,* you know.”

“Who are *you*?” Ella demands. “Why did you bring me here?”

The man runs his hands through his hair until it sticks up even more. Ella’s heart thumps. Had Fiona found out about Ella’s friendship with Amir? Had she plotted all this out of jealousy because the prince liked Ella and not her?

“You?” the man cries. “You? I don’t know you! Where’s Belle? How did you get here?”

Ella swings her leg back over the sill so she’s planted firmly in the room. She places her hands on her hips. This is all too strange for her to feel frightened, at least not yet.

“You didn’t bring me here?” Ella demands. “This isn’t . . . This isn’t a prank?”

“A pr— Oh no,” he whispers. “Oh no. I’m afraid I may have made a terrible mistake.”

2

Belle

A YEAR AGO BELLE WAS KIDNAPPED BY THE Narrow Sea Pirates.

It wasn't as big a deal as it sounds. This type of thing wasn't entirely surprising when your father trades in the rarest, strangest, most extraordinary of magical goods.

And they were nice enough, as far as pirates went, and offered her mulberry cider as they waited for Belle's father. They even gave her a brass spyglass to take home. It really boiled down to a misunderstanding and was easily resolved over tea and Henrik's ginger biscuits.

Which is why Belle knows that she shouldn't be worried now when she wakes to find herself in a fireplace, with a woman and two girls staring down at her. One of them kicks her shins.

This means that *it worked.* Belle's plan *worked.*

Belle pushes herself up, adjusting the sleeves of her shirt and shoving a few unruly locks of brown hair behind her ears, and gives them her biggest grin. She can't believe—well, she should believe, because it *was* such a good idea, but still—*it worked.*

"See," demands the shin-kicker. "I *told* you this wasn't Cinderella."

The woman kneels down next to Belle, a thin pipe between her fingers, smoldering with lemon-smelling smoke. Her hair is brilliantly red with a white stripe on one side, her skin is pale, and even this early in the morning, she shimmers with jewelry: chunks of rubies around her neck, globs of emeralds hanging from her ears, dollops of sapphires on her fingers. A few spidery lines spark outward from the edges of her eyes and pull down the corners of her lips.

Belle stands, shaking out her legs, which are starting to fall asleep. She's in a small cellar where murky light tumbles through a tiny window, like the four of them are deep underwater.

"Where am I?" Belle asks, and then remembers herself. Politeness is always the best sort of diplomacy, either because it makes people happy or because it catches them off guard. "Good morning, by the way."

The woman looks a bit startled but recovers quickly.

"You're in Miravale, my dear. In my cellar." Then she adds, like this should matter to Belle, "I'm Lady Simone Steinem."

It takes all Belle's willpower not to gasp out loud. What she cares about is "Miravale." Hundreds of miles from Belle's home. The city of pink stone, perched above Reverie's northwest coast, where the Revel of Spectacles will take place in two weeks' time.

So Belle's plan 100 percent, absolutely, truly worked.

She fiddles with her locket. It helps her think better, as it always does. It sits warm between her collarbones; it's nearly an extension of her.

"It's a lovely cellar," Belle says, because sometimes being polite requires lying. "But why am I here?"

"I believe that's my question," Lady Simone Steinem says, breathing in smoke from her pipe. "Along with, *Who* are you?"

The woman's two daughters hover behind her, glaring at Belle suspiciously, and Belle mostly ignores them. Sharing Simone's vibrant red hair and wearing billowy nightgowns, they are less tattooed and far less fearsome than pirates.

Belle's question: Why is she in a cellar? The enchantment she used to travel was *supposed* to plop her in Miravale's market square.

Unless . . .

Unless something has gone wrong.

"Where's Ella?" One of the girls chimes in, with

something that looks like chocolate crusted around her mouth. Her hair is a riot of red curls, ineffectively restrained by some ribbons.

"Finally made good on her promise to run away, it seems," Simone sniffs. "And good riddance to that little brat."

"She *was* a brat," says the daughter with long shiny hair and a long narrow nose. "She never put enough honey in my milk, even when I told her to."

"Maybe the beast of the woods got her!" the other daughter exclaims.

"Quiet, Marie. She'd probably terrorize the beast anyway," Simone snaps. "Now. Where were—"

"What are we going to do without a *maid*?" The shiny-haired girl wails, as though she's been told the world is ending.

"Well . . ." Simone's eyes narrow, reminding Belle of a wolf she had seen back home, standing on the edge of a lamb pasture. Belle twirls her locket to calm her nerves.

"I should be going," Belle says quickly. "But my father's a very successful trader. Henrik Villeneuve? Of Villeneuve Trading? To make up for the inconvenience of me showing up in your cellar, he'll be happy to find you . . ." She doesn't like the look in Simone's eyes. "Any—anything you want."

"*Anything* I want?" Simone echoes. "I might want a lot of things."

"Anything," Belle whispers, because Henrik is—was—

capable of granting that, even if bad luck has been plaguing them. With his fleet destroyed so he can't ship goods from elsewhere, and his caravan wrecked so he can't find them himself, maybe *anything* is pushing it a bit far. But Belle's plan will make sure that their next bout of luck is only good.

"Girls." Simone's voice is so saccharine, it makes Belle's jaw ache. "Go upstairs."

Grumbling, the two girls climb up a set of stairs and out of the cellar, and Belle studies the woman again. Her jewels are almost-convincing fakes, but Belle's traveled a lot and learned a lot, which means that Belle knows a lot, even though it sometimes never seems like enough.

"Jewels," Belle blurts. "He could give you a real set of jewels."

Immediately, she knows she's said the wrong thing. The woman's smile tightens, and she takes a long drag from her thin pipe.

"You think you're quite clever, don't you?" The woman's lips peel back. "But what good are jewels going to do me when I don't even have a maid before the Revel of Spectacles?"

No. No. Belle doesn't like where Simone is going with this.

"My father . . . ," she begins.

Simone nods like she's humoring her. "If your father, miracle man that he is, shows up at our doorstep with all you've promised, then you're welcome to leave. But it seems that I'm short some help. And here you are, sitting in her place."

Belle blinks and rubs her locket. It's so preposterous that she thinks she must have misheard. "You . . . You want me to be your maid? Why would I do that?"

"Oh, I'm sure a smart girl like you can think of one reason." Simone snatches Belle's locket, ripping it off before Belle can react. She clasps it around her own neck, straightening. The locket, usually a warm gold, looks faded and flat on Simone's skin.

"What are you *doing*?" Belle gasps. She can't lose the locket. It's the only piece she has of her mother, dead the day Belle was born.

"Being practical," Simone says. "I need a servant until the end of the Revel. You need this." She prods the locket and Belle shivers, like Simone's prodding her.

"You can't do that," Belle retorts, aghast. Belle is used to being called odd, head-in-the-clouds, which is why she's worked hard to be nice, and to prove she's practical and sharp, and to be taken seriously. Not to be trapped in someone's cellar. "You can't force me to be your servant."

"I suppose I have no need for new jewels now, do I?" Simone says, as if Belle hasn't spoken.

The locket is not just a locket. Circular, plain, the gold scratched with age, and looking like nothing special, it possesses a magic so powerful, Belle has been instructed to never ever open it, not unless it's the most important reason in the world.

"You can't do this," Belle chokes out. That locket—it's her family's future.

"All I'm doing is making my own fate. It's a lesson perhaps you should learn." Simone's smile is calm, almost friendly, the way a poisonous flower can seem beautiful. "But you're right. I'll be a little kinder."

Simone kicks over a pail of lentils, scattering them in the fireplace where they mix with the cinders and ash. Belle gapes.

"If you can pick out all the lentils before the clock strikes twelve, I'll give you back your little locket and let you leave." Simone smirks. "Good luck."

Simone strides up the stairs. The cellar door shuts and locks behind her.

3

Ella

BEFORE THIS MAN'S TERRIBLE MISTAKE, and before Ella's father died, and before he married that horrible Simone with her two horrible daughters, Ella used to spend her days beside her father in Miravale's royal library, an enormous underground cavern where fairy lights flickered gold over bookshelves and you could hear the distant whisper of the sea.

Her father, Redmond, was once the royal librarian, and Ella would curl up with old maps as he showed her: *there,* where oceans brewed with sea monsters and sea witches. Or *there,* where doors grew inside trees. When she would demand to see such a place herself, he would sit beside her as they traced out their own maps. Walking home, he would point at the night sky, saying that anyone bold enough to tug on a star would arrive in a place beyond imagination.

Before, Ella had long pale-blond hair that swung like her mother's used to, Redmond had said. No one minded too much that her left leg ended below the knee and that the calf and foot below it were made of glass. It was an enchanted gift her father had searched all of Reverie for, had traded his antique watch, a family heirloom, for.

But then things changed. Redmond married Simone, and things soured at home. A year later, the horrible Miravalian princess made her father lose his post at the library, and coin ran low. And when he fell sick, Ella stayed at his bedside as summer grew heavy, and the fever consumed him. And when grief and panic turned her cold stepmother cruel, and when Fiona started to taunt her, threatening to cut her hair off, Ella grabbed the shears herself. She learned how to sharpen her tongue and cheer herself up by imagining cockroaches in Simone's oats.

But they couldn't take away the one thing she treasured most: the maps that wound through her head. The possibility of adventure.

After Redmond died, Fiona took her bedroom, and Ella moved into the cellar, and Simone filled the house with fake antiques until it was unrecognizable, and the garden shriveled, and Ella was forced to grind the wheat into flour and knead the flour into dough and bake the dough into loaves that were never quite right, wash the towels and hang the sheets on the line and dig dirty socks out from under beds. She scoured the pans and scrubbed the pots, wiped the floors and sudsed the windows, bruised her knuckles and made the knee above her glass leg ache.

She could stop doing chores, move back upstairs, when she was *good,* Simone promised.

And Ella did what Simone asked, because she thought that maybe—maybe things might get better. Simone would see that she *was* trying to be good, she really was, but she couldn't help the anger that burned in her chest at the rotten princess, at her father's illness, at Simone.

Weeks passed, and then months, and then years, and all Ella had was Amir, Miravale's prince, who couldn't understand why she didn't love the city like he did. And Ella grew frustrated wishing on stars for so long without them listening. She promised herself she would run away, find her own adventure, even if she always found an excuse to stop herself from leaving.

Now it seems like she has run away, even if by accident.

"GINGER BISCUIT?"

Ella nods, nibbling at its edges and fidgeting in her seat. The man, Henrik, glugs about a sheep's worth of milk into his tea. He thinks better with tea, he explains, so Ella had turned it down, to avoid thinking better about Simone and how furious she'll be when she realizes Ella is gone.

But . . . what does that anger matter if *Ella is gone*?

Ella decides to accept a cup of tea upon second thought, hiding a gleeful smile behind the teacup and imagining Simone ringing her little bell, demanding toast and coffee, with no one there to answer.

Henrik alternates between shoving a pair of thin wire glasses into his mess of hair and peering through them to study Ella. She wonders what he sees: her blond locks that she's kept chopped above her shoulders, her blue eyes that she got from her father. How the sleeves of her pajamas are stained from the charcoal she uses to sketch maps, how she's a bit pasty, which Simone is constantly criticizing her for, how, if he looked closely, he'd see that part of her is made of glass.

What does he think of all that? She wants to know but is afraid to ask.

"This tea was a gift from a genie in Ambrosia," he says, breathing in the steam. Its sweet, delicate scent is different from the dark, bitter tea of Miravale, though Ella recognizes it from her days at the Miravalian Palace. Queen Milan, Amir's mother, was from Ambrosia and had it imported, and Ella always looked forward to it.

Henrik is a merchant who travels throughout all of Reverie with his daughter, he explains, a once-very-successful merchant who ventured to fantastical realms deep within the Dreamwood—the Ten Falls, the Blue Bear Lakes, Apfel's wyvern nurseries, jungles where rivers tumble with bright pink water. But recently he's been pursued by bad luck, his ships sinking, his caravans breaking, and now his daughter, Belle, vanishing, with Ella in her place at his home in Shepperton, practically on the other side of Reverie from Miravale.

"And that's when I went to get a gift for Belle." Satisfied with his now nearly bone-white tea, Henrik continues. "Belle—well, she's a sharp little thing, and so polite. A dangerous combination. You never can tell exactly what's happening in that head of hers. She hardly ever asks for anything, but then she—the Revel—and I—so . . ." He clears his throat, like there's something he's leaving out.

Henrik frowns at his tea.

"I thought it would be nice to bring her home something special. It's not much. Her mother loved roses, but roses die, so . . . it's just a little clock painted with them." Ella's heart quickens, and her fingers sneak into her pocket, squeezing that exact clock.

Listening to Henrik talk about his daughter makes it unbearable for Ella to give the clock back. She could almost imagine that *her* father had gotten it for *her,* even as she can imagine her father chastising her for letting her imagination bolt away. Again.

Henrik raises his thick eyebrows. "And last night, seeking shelter, I stumbled upon a . . . a nice place. Bit rundown, if we're being honest. And when I saw the clock, I of course thought of Belle . . . and as it happens, I think . . . I think whoever I, erm, *borrowed* it from might not be too . . . too happy about all this."

Ella guesses "borrowed" is the polite word for "stole." Also, it's a clock. All this fuss for a *clock*?

There are plenty more worthwhile things to fuss over here. Henrik's house, a bit lopsided, like a giant picked it up and plopped it back down, is stuffed with items wonderful and strange. The kitchen alone overflows with books that cluck, books covered in fur, snow globes where the people and snowmen inside are moving around, a glass box filled with jeweled beetles, a chessboard where all the pieces are lying down and snoring, a knife broken into three jagged parts with a note that reads *REMINDER: DO NOT FIX. OR ELSE.* Even the kettle does a jig when it whistles.

"You think the person who owns the clock cast a curse?" Ella asks around a ginger biscuit, soft and sweet and spicy. "And stole Belle?"

"As punishment. And you must have gotten caught in the magic." He shakes his head. "A bad curse can be very sloppy. Very sloppy indeed."

Ella licks biscuit crumbs off her fingers. An accidental curse. She doesn't *feel* very cursed.

Henrik leaps up and begins throwing random items into a leather bag, pulling on a patched traveling coat. "I have to get to Belle," he mutters, then pauses, slapping his hand against his forehead. "You need to get home. You said home was Coralon?"

Ella nods at the lie. While Henrik may make good ginger biscuits, he's still a stranger, and she doesn't want to risk that he might know Simone.

And what home really awaits her? Simone and her stepsisters aren't *home.* There's Amir, but he's the prince, and after the last time . . . that horrible, awkward, terrible moment . . . In Miravale, she's just an orphaned scullery maid with half a glass leg.

Your differences make you powerful, her father used to tell her. But what was powerful about a leg that might shatter if you set it down too hard? About being born in a way that made other people believe that maybe you couldn't do as much as you knew you could?

"What if I come with you to help find Belle?" Ella asks, surprising herself. It might have been a misfiring of magic that got her here, but that doesn't mean she can't finally tug a star down and find her own adventure.

"It's too dangerous." Henrik shakes his head. "And your family will be worried."

"They won't be," Ella says. "And I'm not scared."

She's been threatening to run away for months. Simone will think she's finally just gone through with it. Most likely, she'll be panicking that there's no maid. A maid was Simone's proof she was creeping closer to nobility, even if the maid was her stepdaughter, even though the family's coffers only contained cobwebs and memories.

"The person I . . . erm, borrowed . . . from isn't the friendliest sort," Henrik hesitates, and Ella resists the urge to roll her eyes and ask why he even borrowed from that sort of person to begin with, but she's never understood adults and doesn't plan to try now.

"Then you need help," Ella insists. "Please. *I* can help."

Adventure has never been so close. She's not going to let this chance slip through her fingers.

4

Belle

ONE THING BELLE HAS LEARNED IS THAT magic can solve nearly any problem.

Except the problem of not having magic when you need it most.

Over the past hour Belle's tapped the cellar walls to detect hollows, shifted the wine barrels to see if they covered any secret passageways, dug through the fireplace's cinders and the fallen lentils and the pile of dirty laundry to search for a trapdoor. But all she's uncovered are a few maps in some sketchbooks. No way to escape and retrieve the locket. No magical objects tucked away for Belle to use.

If only she'd snagged one of the skeleton keys Henrik kept on the kitchen counter. If only she'd had that old wristwatch that froze time for a few minutes. If only if only if only.

Belle doesn't bother with the lentils. She analyzed it, and it's an impossible task. And impossibilities just mean you have to come up with new ideas.

Already her mind is spinning with one: a wild, ridiculous idea. But sometimes ridiculous is the only way forward, especially in a place like Reverie, where towns have been known to go upside down for a few months and then back to normal, no explanation.

The cellar door cracks open, and the girl with unruly curls slips in. Marie.

"Hi," Marie says. She fiddles with a loose string on her sleeve.

"Hi?" Belle says, but she stops herself before saying anything more. The worst thing she can do is make them wonder why she wants the locket back so badly.

"You didn't pick up the lentils," Marie observes.

Belle shakes her head.

"Mama didn't think you would," Marie says.

"I'm not trying to be difficult," Belle assures her. She wants to be as agreeable as possible, smile her politest, get her locket, and get out of there.

Marie pops a caramel into her mouth and considers Belle. "Then Mama will probably like you more than she liked Ella. You're nicer to her than Ella was."

Belle imagines Ella's attitude might have had something

to do with being forced to be a servant in her own house, but she holds her tongue. Just like she holds her tongue and doesn't say that worrying about having a servant isn't a rational worry. Beasts in the woods or wicked witches infiltrating kingdoms: those are real worries.

Her fingers drift to the spot where her locket used to be. In all her travels across Reverie with her father, she's never lost it. And now, in someone's cellar. Poof. Gone.

"Why are you dressed like that?" Marie asks, pushing through Belle's thoughts. "*Are* you a servant?"

Belle glances down. She'd forgotten that she'd fallen asleep in one of her mother's hand-me-down shirts and pants with plenty of pockets, planning to get up before sunrise and not wanting to bother with pajamas. Her body is marked by adventure: the freckles sprinkled across her nose from a summer spent outside, her nails short (practical), her long wild brown hair yanked back (also practical), the sickle-shaped scar on the inside of her right arm from an encounter with a feisty wyvern. Her gray eyes an heirloom from her mother.

"No," she says. "I'm an explorer. And a trader."

Belle's trying not to be angry or afraid. Whatever situation she's found her way into, there's always a solution.

"Oh. Wow." Marie taps her knuckles against the stone wall. "Why'd you choose to explore our cellar?"

"I . . . didn't," Belle says, not sure if Marie is serious. She can't be serious. But she seems to be, her eyes wide, her mouth slightly open.

"Then why are you here?" Marie wonders. "What did you do with Ella? *Did* you send her into the woods? Turn her into a mouse?"

"I don't know Ella." Belle's fingers drift up to her neck where her locket is supposed to hang. "And I wouldn't turn anyone into a mouse."

"Are you a witch?" Marie pries. "Is this magic?"

Yes, magic that's gone wrong. But Belle's determined to make it right.

Marie bobs her shoulders. "If I had magic," she says piously, "I would turn *everyone* into mice."

ONCE MARIE HAS RUSHED AWAY, REALIZING SHE forgot what she came to tell Belle in the first place, Belle scrunches her nose and tries to think where the world might have gone sideways.

Before she ended up here, she and her father had been home in Shepperton, a tiny village within the kingdom of Apfel, with wooden houses, roads that turned muddy in the rain, and people arguing over the price of bread and eggs. It was cradled by rolling green hills where sheep grazed and geese roosted. It was as pretty as a painting—and as boring, if Belle was being honest.

Whenever she was home, she tore through everything the bookstore had to offer and spent most of her time trying to ignore the matrons who scolded and said pants were meant for boys, or trying to befriend the village girls who made an equally great effort to avoid her.

The Villeneuve house was tiny and lopsided, tucked on the far edge of town, which was probably a reason the villagers found Belle and Henrik odd, though certainly not the only one.

Belle and Henrik were rarely at home, usually criss-crossing Reverie to sell and acquire magical goods. But a week ago one of the wheels on their caravan broke, and then Henrik was hit by the news that the last ship of his dwindling fleet had sunk.

Which is when Belle came up with her plan: the Revel of Spectacles.

Miravale's Revel of Spectacles is a two-week-long festival that ripples through the city, with smaller celebrations popping up throughout Reverie. One hasn't happened in years, not since King Phillip and Queen Milan got married. Now one was being held for Crown Prince Amir Perrault's thirteenth birthday, per Miravalian tradition.

That's not what Belle cares about.

She cares about what happens on the night of the first day. The prince hosts a competition for people throughout Reverie, and the winner receives a royal favor. No one can predict what the competition will be, but every Revel, the royal favor changes the winner's life. Erases debts, builds homes, invests in new crops for ailing farms, provides scholarships.

Hers was a perfect plan, Belle knows, because knowing is what Belle does best. She's going to win the Revel's competition and restore her family's fortunes.

She's been reading about puzzles and quests in anticipation. She's practiced how to talk to spiders and how to mix together healing herbs and how to see in the dark.

And if all else fails, Belle has a secret weapon.

Her locket.

It was passed down to Belle from her mother, Cora, who received it from her mother, who received it from hers, and on and on, making its way through the generations. When opened, the locket could erase any magical spell or calm any magical creature, a power so rare and potent that even Henrik had only heard rumblings of similar objects. It hadn't been enough to save her mother, but it will save Belle and her father now. Revels tend to include difficult magic traps or puzzles, like figuring out how to open an enchanted door or face an enchanted beast.

Using the locket was out of the question for Henrik; it was all they had left of her mother. No reward was great enough to merit destroying it. And besides, he wouldn't let Belle put herself in danger. The last Revel of Spectacles ended in a tangle with wild trolls. And when Belle reminded him about the pirates, he said those were calculated risks and it had ended up all right, hadn't it? And they would figure it out. They always did.

The locket is Belle's calculated risk. She can't spend

another day watching her father worry about bills due, his usual smile vanished. Between Belle's cleverness and the locket's power, she'll be able to win the Revel's competition.

The night before Belle had woken up in a fireplace, Henrik had set off on a horse to meet someone who wanted a magical snow globe, commanding Belle to stay at home until his return the following day.

"I'll bring you something," he promised. "What would you like?"

A peace offering, she knew, for not letting her go to the Revel.

"A rose," she decided, because they couldn't afford much else, and roses had been her mother's favorite flower.

Once he was gone, she promptly disobeyed him and picked up the pirate's bronze spyglass. The Revel was more than a week away, but she wanted time in case she got lost or could pick up hints about what the competition entailed. The spyglass was enchanted, allowing the user to leap across great distances, and the pirates had given her detailed instructions. She angled it mostly west and a little north toward Miravale and thought, *Revel, Revel, Revel.*

And then she woke up *here.*

Inside the cellar, where—

It's starting to rain.

Belle spins around, trying to find leaking water, but all that accompanies the sound is the air shimmering, rainbow-streaked.

A man appears in the center of the cellar, dipping into a low bow. He's dressed so brightly that Belle is almost blinded. His waistcoat and shirt and pants and nail polish are all the same brilliant blue. He has silver hair smoothed back and teeth as white as clouds, and Belle feels a surge of relief. He can't be anything but a fairy.

"I am your fairy godfather," he declares with a flourish. "And I'm here to help you leave this drab and sorry life behind, my darling Ella."

"You mean Belle," Belle supplies helpfully. Maybe Henrik has sent the fairy godfather. A few fairies do owe him favors.

The fairy godfather's brow furrows. He pulls out a small mirror from his breast pocket and studies it, clucking his tongue against the back of his teeth.

"Does Belle happen to be a nickname?" he asks. "For . . . Ella?"

"Belle's a nickname for Belle," Belle says. "But similar enough, right?"

"And you haven't . . . You haven't happened to see a beast about?"

"A *beast*?" Belle asks. "There's a *beast* here?"

He makes a face. "This is awkward," he says. "Awkward indeed. But it seems there's been a teensy bit of a mistake. And these things do happen, once in a while. So. Sorry about that, my dear." He pats her on the head. "Good luck with all this."

The air around him starts to shimmer again.

"What *is* all this?" Belle cries out, but her hand clasps only empty air.

The fairy godfather is gone, and Belle slumps against the wall, gazing at the spot where he disappeared in case another fairy takes his place, lined up for duty.

If the fairy godfather was trying to transport Ella out of here and Belle was trying to transport herself *to* Miravale—had their magic collided, distorting the other?

It's not improbable. She's heard of similar things. Maybe Ella would wake up in Belle's house, and Henrik will figure out that Belle is in Miravale. With Henrik's knowledge of Reverie's secret pathways and shortcuts, he'll be here soon.

And Henrik will take her back to Shepperton.

And she won't be able to participate in the Revel of Spectacles.

Belle didn't attempt transportation magic and have her plans derailed by someone else's fairy godfather just to go back *home.* All she has to do is get the locket, and the rest will be easy.

No matter what the competition throws at her—Belle hopes it's a puzzle, ideally one with riddles or spider-talking—she knows the locket and its magic will help her prevail. After all, Belle has seen many magical things, and nothing has felt quite like the locket, warm and comforting against her skin, the way hope feels.

The cellar door cracks open.

It's Marie again. This time, lugging a big bucket that she plops down with a sigh.

"They give me the worst chores." Marie taps the side of the bucket with her foot. "She said to start preparing dinner."

"Dinner?" Belle asks.

Marie nudges the bucket again. A terrible, awful smell fills Belle's nose.

"Yuck," Marie says. "Ella'd always tie a rag around her nose, if that helps."

She slams the door behind her, leaving Belle alone with the stench and only a sliver of sunlight.

Belle peeks into the bucket. It's full of marble-eyed fish, with a note reading *Gut them.*

She needs magic. But it won't be easy to find with the Steinems hovering around her.

Tapping the spot where her locket is supposed to hang, Belle thinks she might have preferred pirates.

5

Ella

ELLA CLINGS TO THE HORSE AS IT GALLOPS down the dirt road through the farmlands, her fingers wrapped into its mane and her thighs clenching its sides.

"Gallops" might be an exaggeration.

Since they've left Henrik's house, the horse has been barely trotting, but it's enough for Ella. Next time she starts an adventure, she'll do it on foot. Her knee aches. Her stomach twists and spins.

Henrik draws his own horse to a pause and looks back at her. The wind has disheveled his white hair even more, so it looks like he's been struck by lightning, and the summer sun has flushed his face.

"Are you okay?" he calls.

She nods, afraid that her voice will come out rickety, and she doesn't want to bother him any more. He's already given her, to replace her pajamas, a clean blue dress that's a tad too big—"Belle doesn't wear them anyway"—and a pair of shoes.

Ella rubs the top of her knee. This time Henrik notices.

"Your leg?" he asks. He returns to her and begins rummaging through his leather bag, little bottles clinking. "Here. I'm sure I have— Why, yes. Here."

He holds out a small silver pot.

"You won't need much," he instructs. "A dab at the end of your pinky."

Ella hesitates. But there's no joke, no punch line, like there would be with her stepfamily. Just a man with an offer.

"Sometimes we all just need a little hope," he says.

"There's hope in here?" Ella asks, her mind starting to whir the way it does whenever she gets close to magic.

Henrik's face lights up. "Just a dab," he encourages. "Wonderful little potion, isn't it?"

Ella unscrews the lid. The substance shimmers like opals and feels like summer mornings. She tugs down her stocking and rubs it against the spot where her leg becomes glass. Immediately it feels better.

"I recognize this leg." Henrik's eyes meet hers. "I traveled very far to bring it back to a librarian. For his daughter."

Ella's heart races. Impossible . . . but possible. Henrik's

talking about her father, and he's talking about her. He must be the merchant her father bought her leg from.

"He's dead," Ella says sharply. "He died."

Henrik's face falls. "I'm sorry, my dear. He was a good man."

Ella looks away. She feels strange. Henrik is carrying memories of her father, just as she is. And without Henrik, she wouldn't have a leg.

They continue near fields, farmers lounging near cows or bent over berry bushes, baby manticores chirping from behind fences. Ella has to constantly stop herself from gasping at all the things she hasn't seen, starving for more and more and more.

They pause near the edge of the farmland. Before them, maple trees sweep up to the sky—the beginning of the Dreamwood, which takes up the center of Reverie. Where magic reigns freely. Where some of the most thrilling of stories live, and also the most dangerous.

There had been reports in Miravale about murderous goblins that lurked outside city walls, promising to tell people secrets and luring them into the Dreamwood instead. And, of course, there's the beast of the woods. They said that the beast caught travelers and kidnapped maidens; some even said that's why the Miravalian princess disappeared, although the royal-approved story was that she was sent to live with an aunt near the Eastern Sea. Petty precautions had gripped Miravale since: hanging rosemary by your door to keep the beast away, carrying silver daggers if you left the city walls.

Ella glances at Henrik. Surely Henrik will know if something is too dangerous. He's an adult. Adults are boringly careful.

"You're sure you want to come?" Henrik asks, nodding at the woods. "There is no shame in turning back. We can arrange a carriage home for you in Shepperton that goes on safer routes than this."

"I'm not turning back," Ella declares, gripping the pony's saddle so tightly with worry that her knuckles pop white. "But . . . do you have any rosemary?"

Henrik guffaws. "Rosemary? And what do you intend to do with that? Season some trout?"

Ella rolls her eyes. She *knew* that had to be a superstition.

The path winds beyond the first tree, and Ella braces herself for monstrous spiders, robber barons, hulking ogres, but—there's nothing frightening about the Dreamwood. It's sun-dappled and as fresh as spring. Tiny creatures scurry in the ferns, massive tulips and sunflowers burst along the path, and maple leaves twist red and gold in the breeze.

Ella's never known an excitement like this, bubbling in her chest. She's in the *Dreamwood,* a place she's only seen on maps!

Soon the path narrows, and every few feet it splits off

into three different routes. But Henrik never hesitates, turning left and then right, and then center, and then left again. If they were separated, Ella isn't sure she'd ever find her way back out.

"Hold your breath," Henrik says, and there's a second where Ella feels like she's being squeezed through a tube, and the woods distort, the trees as skinny as Simone's pipe and as tall as palaces. Then— "There we are!" Henrik crows, sounding delighted. "That's a handy little shortcut, if you know your way around. Didn't lose any fingers, did you?"

Ella checks. All ten fingers appear present. The woods are back to normal, summer swooning, but here, all the flowers are gentle baby's breath and triumphant foxglove, the maples replaced by spruces that are tall and thick and resilient. It smells minty with evergreens.

They're now just a bit southeast of Miravale, Henrik explains, and Ella tries to make sense of this; they've zipped countless miles in a second. She wishes she had her sketchbook. How do you map a shortcut that defies logic? How do you map magic?

They continue trotting forward. Moss dangles in lacy sheaths from tree branches. Butterflies as big as birds flutter next to sparrows that look like they're made of water and trill songs that sound like—

A wall of rosebushes rears just beyond them, with thorns as long as knives and a few white flowers floating deep within the bramble.

The castle emerges before them as quickly as a crash, its arched windows and pointed spires emerging from beyond the wall of roses. It's all white wood and white stone, with dark metal sketched along its sides like the veins on a leaf. What appears to be snow flurries surround it, despite it being the depths of summer.

Something isn't right.

The woods have fallen silent, Ella realizes. The birdsong has vanished. Branches continue to shiver in the wind, but there's no sound of rustling ferns or pine needles. It's like sound has abandoned this place. Maybe she should have thought a little bit more carefully before volunteering to come.

"Not many people make it here," Henrik says with a touch of pride. "Magic keeps the castle hidden, unless you know its exact location. Or you get lucky."

"How did you find it?"

"Finding what's not supposed to be found is my job," Henrik says, and Ella feels a swell of awe and envy. She wants to find things that can't be found, create maps that defy existence. "And I got lucky."

The horses' hooves don't make any noise against the dirt path. Ella whistles under her breath, and the notes are immediately snatched away. Her stomach churns. What kind of magic steals sound?

Probably not the good kind, she thinks.

Noise returns as they reach the gate, although still no birds sing. "We'll leave the boys here," Henrik says as they reach a pair of wrought iron gates nearly buried within the brambles. They dismount their horses, and Ella helps tie them up. The animals are restless, pawing at the ground, and they only calm when Henrik draws blindfolds over their eyes.

Before Henrik can touch the gates, they swing open.

Henrik hesitates, and Ella hesitates, and there's something here that makes her skin prickle with dread. She imagines she's in one of her father's stories, a warrior princess come to vanquish a dragon and free a maiden. Or steal its treasure. Ella wouldn't mind some treasure.

She charges forward, leaving Henrik no choice but to follow.

As soon as they step through the gates, the summer warmth vanishes, replaced by winter's chill. Snowflakes drift about them, and goose bumps prickle on Ella's arms. Everything is white with frost: the hedges, the stone pathway, the hydrangea bushes, the thatched roof of the stables, a fountain with a statue of a wolf. A lake is frozen over.

The closer they get to the castle, the more foreboding it looks, windowsills rotting and windows dark, ivy creeping up stones scarred with neglect. Ella gulps, imagining Belle waking up here. She hopes it's nicer inside, for her sake.

Ella and Henrik keep going closer.

Odd clumps of cream-white pomegranates hang from snow-frosted branches overhead, sending off a sugary smell. Ella's fingers drift toward them.

"Don't pick anything," Henrik warns, and she brings her arms toward her sides. "This is a cursed place."

Cursed.

At his words, the castle's massive doors fling open. Ella gasps—she can't help it. The entryway is gloomy and grand, with thick pillars, a fireplace as big as a man, and a stairway that sweeps into shadows. A massive chandelier dangles overhead, coated in dust.

"Where is my daughter?" Henrik challenges the empty castle.

"There's no one here," Ella says, tugging on his sleeve.

"Just because you can't see something doesn't mean it's not there," Henrik whispers out of the corner of his mouth.

Some*one,* Ella wants to correct, not some*thing,* but then—it can't be. The *castle* starts to hiss. The sound grows from a teapot's whistle to an angry kitten to what Ella can only imagine comes from a snake so large, it could wrap around the entire building.

She gulps.

"Thief." The hiss turns into a bellow, echoing around them. "Return what you stole."

"I'll return what's yours when you return what's mine," Henrik declares, and Ella is impressed by how tall he stands, even when his hands are trembling, sweat crowning his brow. "It seems I'm not the only thief."

"I have nothing of yours," the voice threatens. "And I don't deal with liars."

"Where is Belle?" Henrik cries.

"I know no Belle," the voice hisses.

"Who's the liar now?" Henrik challenges, but Ella has a sinking feeling that wherever Belle is, it's not here. Ella wonders miserably why they hadn't considered less terrifying options first, like Ella's cellar.

"I won't listen to your accusations, thief." A low roar rips through the air, and the entire castle trembles. Ella wraps her arms around herself.

"I'm not a— Let me leave, and I'll come back with it. It's nothing compared to Belle," he swears, becoming more desperate. "I'll bring it to you, and you'll tell me where Belle is."

Ella's fingers trip guiltily over the clock's smooth wood, still tucked in her pocket. When Henrik explained all this, he left out the bit about the monster.

"I don't let thieves leave with their hands or liars leave with their tongues," the voice thunders. "But you? I won't allow you to leave at all."

Henrik gasps, falling to his knees, and Ella's head clangs. All she can think of are thunderstorms.

When her father was already starting to fall ill, he had taken her to a local bookseller to wander the shelves. On the way home the sky ripped open, lightning clashed, and wind churned. Without a thought Redmond passed his cloak to one of the street orphans huddling beside the buildings. Her father had done it without question; it was simply the right thing to do.

Which is why Ella acts without thinking, as surprised

as Henrik when she steps in front of him and declares, "Take me instead."

"What? Ella, no," he whispers. "You can't do this."

Terror prickles the back of Ella's neck. She's read enough books, heard enough stories to know that adventure doesn't start by shrinking away from it.

But more than that, Henrik helped her and her father years ago. He found her a leg. Ella wants to be the kind of girl that her father expected her to grow up to be. And all she's done is sit in the corner of a cellar and dream.

Ella tugs the clock out of her pocket.

Henrik gasps. Even the hissing voice seems like it's holding its breath.

"I was the one who stole it," she lies. "Not him."

"What are you doing?" Henrik whispers.

"I'm the . . ." She clears her throat, her words catching with nervousness. "I'm the thief. Give him . . . Give him back his daughter."

"I have no daughter of his," the voice growls.

"Don't do this, Ella," Henrik begs.

Ella is tired of bullies. After so long serving Simone, she can't tolerate more unjust punishments and cruelty. And surely the voice won't keep her long, right? Once they realize she's just a girl trying to help a father?

"Take me." Ella's surprised that her words don't waver even as her heart hammers.

The voice hesitates, then mutters, "Be gone, merchant. Be grateful I'm letting you leave."

"No!" Henrik cries, but something moves so quickly, Ella can't see what it is, grabbing Henrik by the back of his shirt and flinging him out the doors, back into the path of pomegranate trees and the waiting woods.

"Go find Belle!" Ella cries. *And come back for me,* she pleads in her head.

"Ella!" he shouts. "I won't forget this!"

Too late, Ella wonders if she's made a terrible mistake. Too late, she realizes she never told Henrik she was from Miravale so he'll know that's where Belle might be.

Fear knocks through her like a bird rattling in a cage.

The doors slam shut, and the castle plunges into darkness.

6

Belle

THE NEXT MORNING MARIE IS BACK WITH another bucket of fish.

Belle is cross-legged on the bed, flipping through the maps of Reverie that Ella left behind. There are a few errors, sure—clearly, Ella hasn't ever actually been to Cypress Grove, or she'd know that Troll Canyon is much farther away—but Belle is impressed.

If Henrik knew where she was, he would have arrived in Miravale by now, or at least sent letters or guards. She can only assume somewhere in Reverie, he must be lost trying to find her. Belle's not worried—Henrik always gets out of trouble—and this could be a good thing. She'll escape with the locket, proving to her father that she can handle herself. That she can and should compete in the Revel.

"Sorry." Marie wrinkles her nose as she drops the fish bucket to Belle.

Belle's body aches from all of yesterday's sweeping and dusting and rug-shaking and pot-scrubbing and silver-shining, done without complaint to stay on Simone's good side. Fiona had spent most of the day hovering about her, delightedly criticizing everything Belle did while rattling away about how she was going to marry the prince.

"Prince Amir will probably propose on a boat ride near the Amorous Falls," she had declared, along with about a hundred other locations.

As she thinks about that, Belle decides that maybe her mind aches, too.

Marie slides the bucket forward. "At least no one will bother you today," she says. "Mother's taking us shopping for the Revel."

Belle hides a smile behind one of Ella's maps.

It's time to put her plan into action.

BELLE SCALES THE FISH, AND LISTENS.

She trims the fish, and listens.

She guts the fish, and listens, and feels grateful the pirates taught her what to do with a bucket of fish.

And finally, by the time she's scrubbed fish scales out

from underneath her nails, there's the clatter of Simone and her daughters in the room above Belle.

Simone's sharp heels descend down the stairs to the cellar.

"No funny business while we're gone," Simone commands, poking her head into the cellar before locking the door behind her.

Belle isn't worried about locks. When finally, finally, finally there's the slamming of the front door and the silence of an empty house, Belle hops onto the bed and cracks open the little window above it.

She sticks her arms out, digging her fingers into the grass outside for extra leverage, and she grits her teeth as she squeezes through the narrow opening.

Now Belle flops into a very sad, scraggly garden—"garden" is a kind word, given that little seems to grow—and leaps to her feet, brushing strands of grass and dirt off her borrowed dress. Simone had forced one of Ella's old dresses onto her, a bit too short for Belle and as much of a sack as a dress could be.

Belle hurries out the back gate and onto the street, surprised by how *ordinary* the Steinems' town house looks. It's like every other house on the street, the same pink stone, the same tiled roof, the same large bundle of dried rosemary hung near the front door to protect against the beast of the woods that's been said to be threatening Miravale.

Belle scoffs. She wonders what alchemist made that lie up to sell more rosemary.

Finding her way is easy. Even if Belle hadn't visited Miravale before with her father, the streets are wide and nearly all lead to the Miravalian Palace, which stands on a hill slightly above the city, its blushing pink towers a beacon. Inside is Belle's destination: the Workshop, where magic is brewed in bottles and test tubes. Nothing humans create is as strong as what fairies or witches can brew up, but the Miravale Palace doesn't employ many magical folk, and all Belle needs is a simple calling spell to help her locket return to her.

No one pays much attention to Belle as she navigates the busy streets, but Belle pays attention to them. The streets burble with rumor and speculation of the Revel's competition, with anticipations of glory and heroics.

"Do you think they'll have to find jewels?"

"They had to find that tiara last time."

"Do you think they'll have to go into the catacombs?"

"They went into the *catacombs* the time before that."

"Who says that they can't do the same thing again?"

"Maybe it'll be a maze."

"It was a maze the time *before* the time before last time."

"Are you going to enter?"

"Are you?"

"Well . . . if I won, I'd have them put statues of me in every market."

"The only way *you'd* win is if the rest of the contestants were turned into toads."

Belle struggles to resist making faces as she passes the people.

She could run away. Right now. Leave Simone and all her nonsense behind. But . . . But while the Miravalian people might want to win the wrong things, they have the right idea. The competition is unpredictable, with unpredictable magic. She needs the locket to make sure she emerges victorious.

And besides, she's had that locket her whole life, and Henrik would be heartbroken if she lost it. She would be, too.

By the time Belle has arrived at the Miravalian Palace, her mind is buzzing. She can outsmart puzzles and competitors, she can dodge and outrun strong men, and with the locket, she can probably face down any enchantments. With it, victory is assured. With it, it's like her mother's there, protecting her.

Belle's so deep in her thoughts that she bumps into a group of tourists gawking at the Miravalian Sunrise Garden in front of the palace. Statues of daring knights and waving kings and swooning princesses hold court among the lilac trees and marigolds.

The Miravalian Palace is a tufted cake of a castle, with pink stone walls and stained glass windows and balustrades and bridges strung between towers. Its spires twirl high into the air, capped with steep copper roofs.

Sometimes there's no better disguise than being what everyone thinks you are: a girl touring a castle.

The Great Hall is bustling with the occasional magical folk from the Dreamwood and primarily Miravalian elite in velvet finery with pointed shoulders, sipping from dainty teacups or perched on chaise longues before three-tiered silver trays of cakes. There are giant glass vases of wisteria, small streams that run through the halls. Light spills in candy colors, and a string quartet plays a lively waltz, although no one dances.

Belle doesn't have time for pretty things, not as she glimpses a door on the second floor belching multicolored steam. She scurries up one of the spiral staircases, dodging a courtier with a purple wig shaped like a beehive.

Belle has to dodge a cluster of girls fawning before a portrait of Prince Amir, with his careless smile and wind-tousled dark hair. One girl explains how she's going to trick him into marriage, and another clutches her chest, swearing she's going to *pass out if I see him.* It seems Fiona has some competition.

Belle certainly doesn't have time for princes as she stops in front of the arched entryway: the Workshop. Another wave of bright green steam sweeps outward and over Belle. She takes a step forward and sways on her feet, feeling sickeningly dizzy. . . .

She pinches the inside of her arm to steady herself as a man who has thick blond curls and is wearing bug-eyed goggles stumbles out, waving his hand in front of his face and coughing.

"I said *not* to use the willow root, you nincom—"

The man stops short, noticing Belle, who's sagged

against one of the pink walls, eyes shut tight to ward off the nausea.

"Oh," he tuts, shaking his head. "This is why I told them to keep the Workshop far from visitors."

He digs smelling salts out from his pocket and waves them under Belle's nose. The dizziness passes, and she coughs at the sharp odor.

"The liability," the man mutters, glancing down into the Great Hall, where a few people are still looking up with appreciation, a few clapping, like the green smoke was all for show. "I swear. As if what happened with Little Red wasn't enough of a reminder."

With the smoke cleared, Belle can see inside the Workshop: Several other researchers and apprentices are tossing goggles aside and rubbing their eyes, pushing themselves up from where they had passed out onto a massive stone counter that runs down the middle of the room. Smaller counters cling to the walls, where cauldrons puff, tools clang, a very expensive-looking sword has been taken to pieces, and vials swish with liquid that looks alive.

Though Belle has always yearned to explore the Workshop, she turns to the man.

"I'm looking for the Translator," she says.

The man shoves his goggles onto his blond locks.

"You're Cora and Henrik's girl, aren't you? Belle?" he asks. "There's a little bit of both of them in you. His smile. Her eyes."

Belle nods. "You're the Translator?"

Usually, Translators are creatures shaped by their work, bodies hunched and thin from years crouched over Reverie's most ancient and dangerous texts, unscrambling their secrets. They give up their names to disappear into their calling and are said to have fingernails as long as knives to handle more delicate pages, skin pale from years without seeing the sun, and eyes that go blind from words not meant to be read by humans.

"Translating is a noble calling," this Translator says with a heavy sigh, "but when you work for a royal family, you spend more time overseeing the execution of translations than doing any actual translating. Probably better for my eyes, as it is. Now. Is your father around?"

"You're making a sleeping spell?" Belle asks, changing the subject. She'd love to help Simone enjoy a nice, long nap, but as far as she knows, only one very cruel witch was able to create such a spell.

"Unfortunately. There have been rumblings about that sleeping curse that happened centuries ago, and it gave the queen the idea. A supposed way to deal with this goblin business without actually hurting them. All we've managed to do is cause a little dizzy spell." The Translator rubs his neck. "But, my dear, what brings you here?"

In the laboratory a young woman with her black hair pulled back frowns over a glass platter filled with what looks like lizard eyeballs. It takes all Belle's willpower to not barge in and ask what she's doing.

Belle stands taller, so the Translator will take her more seriously as she asks, "I need a calling potion. Please."

"Where is your father?" the Translator asks again, his eyes narrowing. "Where's Henrik?"

He doesn't look angry, only worried. Which frustrates Belle, that people assume that if she's by herself, she's in trouble.

"It's a long story," she says. "And I'll tell you all of it. Just . . . not now. Can you help me? Please?"

"We can't give out potions without authorizations," the Translator says. "Especially not ones that have a history of being used in the criminal arts."

Belle has to stop herself from grinding her teeth. She had forgotten how strict Miravale could be. Sure, the castle was open to visits from magical folk, but magic was still treated with distrust.

"It's really important," Belle insists.

The Translator glances around them, eyes narrowing.

"Is Miravale in danger?" he whispers.

Belle frowns. "Not exactly."

"Is *Reverie* in danger?"

"Well . . . not exactly."

"Is it Henrik?" the Translator asks, alarmed.

"Yes," Belle says.

Belle tries not to lie, because there's enough zaniness in the world that adding lies just makes it unnecessarily complicated.

This is, technically, kind of, not a lie.

"Oh. Oh no." The Translator drops his voice again. "Is he okay?"

"Yes," Belle hurries, not wanting to cause undue worry. "But I really need a—"

Somehow, even from up here, with its myriad of scents and sounds, Belle catches a whiff of lemon smoke.

Belle peers over the railing, back into the Great Hall, where a red-haired woman stands commandingly in front of the doors, in a velvet dress and jewels so green, they look like a frog got seasick. Behind her Fiona simpers, and Marie is trying to beckon over one of the castle dogs without her mother and sister noticing.

Belle stifles a groan.

"Can you get me something *now*?" Belle asks.

"Now?" the Translator repeats. "I'm sorry, my dear. Without explicit permission from the king and queen, we can't give out any enchantments more potent than one to relieve indigestion. There are a lot of regulations around lab-made magic. And that's a good thing, you see," the Translator continues.

On to plan B.

If only Belle had a plan B. She'd really been counting on this.

Her attention falls to the floor below.

Simone is sashaying forward—to the stairs.

Belle takes stock. There's only one set of stairs, as far as Belle can see. She can't risk getting into trouble for exploring a palace, or having Simone reach the house before her and realizing she's gone.

So Belle rearranges her hair to curtain her face and hurries past Simone, who has fallen deep into conversation with a courtier and her daughters.

"It's disgusting, truly, they let that *lab* be here." Simone gestures toward the Workshop. "Next thing you know, this place will be swarming with rats."

Belle glances back only once, as Simone's eyes flick toward her, and she sees Simone's brow knotted with questions.

If Simone asks, Belle will claim she was in the cellar all day.

And she's thought of another idea. This one just might be a little messier.

7

Ella

AS SOON AS THE DOORS SLAM SHUT, SOMEthing pins Ella's arms behind her, tearing the clock away and lifting her halfway into the air. Her toes drag against the flagstone corridors as she is rushed along. The entire castle is pitched in darkness, like an inkwell had been tipped over it.

Ella is jolted as her captor descends some stairs, and the chill and the heavy scent of mold and wet fur thicken as she is tossed unceremoniously into a cell.

Here, the dark becomes darker than Ella knew darkness could be, not even a scrap of light to help Ella's eyes adjust.

"Let me out!" Ella cries, rattling the bars.

No one answers.

Ella paces. And paces. And paces. Within the small cell her bad knee is starting to ache again, and she can't take more than two steps before bumping into a slimy wall or the cold steel bars. Her mouth and nose are full of a damp, musty smell.

Eventually, she dozes, on and off, even when she tells herself she won't. When she wakes, there's no way to tell the passing of time. The dark remains, and by now a day could be gone. Or weeks. Her stomach suggests weeks.

"I'll . . . I'll curse you!" Ella declares. "I'm a very dangerous witch!"

No one answers.

Ella pats her pockets to see if there's anything in them that might be useful. A feather she picked up that might prove to be magical, or even a little penknife that she could try to wriggle into the lock. But Ella's pockets are empty. A witch would probably be more prepared for this situation.

The one thing she tries not to do is *wish,* in case a fairy overhears her.

Most fairies like tricks and riddles. They like to muddle things, so you end up with a baby's head when you wish for eternal youth or a very amorous toad when you wish for true love.

"You can't keep me locked up here forever!" Ella tries again.

"Good morning."

Ella jumps. The voice comes from straight in front of her, although she can't see anything through the gloom. It's not the hissing voice from before, but as with anything unseen, it's still frightening.

"What's it they say about time flying when you're having fun?" Ella quips.

"It was just overnight," the voice snips. "Not forever. And you were asleep most of the time."

The truth is, Ella's terrified. Fear is lodged in her throat like a hair ball, and her mouth is so dry, she's worried the words won't come out right. But what's worse than fear is letting other people know you're afraid. She learned that from Simone.

"It's not *so* bad in here, is it?" the voice says. It almost sounds worried, as though she's supposed to find it cozy. Ella blinks into the dark.

"It would only be better if I were surrounded by hungry sharks," Ella says dryly.

Her father had once told her that her sharp tongue would get her into trouble, but talking boldly made her feel bolder, and with Simone, words had become her only weapons. That, and being as bad at her chores as she could be without Simone throwing a tantrum.

"Is that so?" the voice asks, and it almost sounds curious. "Do you know where you are, prisoner?"

"I'm guessing I didn't get lucky enough for the sharks?" Ella asks.

The voice coughs and says, "You are a prisoner of the beast of the woods."

Ella's knees go weak.

No. That can't be true.

There is not a soul in Miravale, and perhaps not in Reverie, that doesn't harbor a fear of the beast of the woods. Even Simone hangs dried sprigs of rosemary from the front door to keep the beast at bay. Though there have been rumors that the beast spun magic around its lair to make it impossible to find, Queen Milan has forbid any hunter or aspiring hero from going after it, for facing a beast so fearsome can only result in certain death.

Henrik wouldn't have stolen from *that* beast of the woods. He couldn't be that foolish.

Her heart knocks against her ribs.

"Ah," the voice says when she doesn't respond. "So you are familiar with the stories."

"It'll be a great story to tell back home," she manages to say, willing her voice not to tremble.

"Oh. Oh. I'm very sorry to disappoint," the voice says, sounding genuinely sorry. "But you won't be going home."

Ella feels dizzy and freezing all at once. This isn't the type of adventure she wanted.

"So," the voice continues. "From where did you steal the clock?"

"The . . . the clock?"

"Yes. From which room did you steal it?"

Her mind buzzing with fear, Ella tries to untangle the question. Is it worse to be a thief, or worse to be a liar?

"From the . . . the library?" is all she can manage. Henrik seems like the type of man to go straight for a library.

And an honest thief, she thinks, can repent. Maybe she'll be granted mercy.

"You lied," the voice marvels. "You *lied*. That's great news!"

"Define 'lie,'" Ella says.

"No one has been in our library in years," the voice says. "And even if someone had, that clock has been in one room only. *Not* the library."

So dishonest non-thief it's going to be, then. Ella isn't sure what she's expecting, but it's not for the voice to whisper, "Open," and for the cell door to obey with a creak.

"Here." There's a rattle, a brief flicker of light. A tray is shoved into the cell, a small candle glimmering next to a pewter bowl filled with what looks like it came out of the back end of a goat.

"Who are you? What's going to happen to me?" Ella asks.

"Close," the voice commands.

The door swings shut again. The voice clears its throat.

"I," the voice announces, "am Sir Stanley von Wensilus VonTrapp Hagenauer Halstatt the Third, though usually my position is much more important than fraternizing with prisoners." Each word comes out louder than the next, like the voice is trying to make a point it's not completely convinced of. "And who are you?"

"Ella Aberdeen." Or is that a bad idea, to tell mysterious voices your name? Too late. "What's going to happen to me?"

"*Dinner,* Ella," he declares, and Ella wishes there was a little bit more clarity on whether he means the bowl of mush, or if *she* is going to be dinner.

The voice quiets without a goodbye. Ella waits. She waits a decent amount of time. She takes a hesitant bite of the mush and is surprised it doesn't taste *as* terrible as it could.

And when she's sure that the voice is gone, she doesn't let herself worry about bad ideas. She's not spending another moment in the dark, waiting for someone to decide she's next on the menu.

Grabbing the candle, she slinks to the door and whispers, "Open." It waits a second, as though it's doubtful it should obey but isn't actually sure what to do with prisoners. The lock clicks and Ella slips through.

And, best as she can with her glass leg, she runs.

8

Belle

BELLE LIES ON HER STOMACH ON THE CELlar floor, lining up fish heads.

"C'mon," she whispers. "Here, little rats. Come here."

This maybe isn't her most sophisticated moment. Or one of her better-smelling ones.

But it's almost the evening of her second day here. And she was supposed to be gone. Done. Locket in hand, preparing for the Revel, dodging Henrik. But there's still no sign of him, which doesn't entirely surprise Belle. He has an affinity for getting lost.

It's not like Belle was planning to rely on rodents, but when all you have is a bucket of fish heads and desperation, this is what you get.

"Belle?"

Marie hovers at the cellar door, and then, like she had an internal debate with herself, marches in.

Belle leaps upright, brushing dirt off her apron and jamming her hands in her pockets in case there are still scales underneath her nails. But there's nothing she can do about the row of fish heads lined up behind her, like soldiers preparing for battle.

"I'm *starving,*" Marie says. She pops a maple candy into her mouth, her words slipping around it. "Mama made us have tea at the castle but wouldn't let us eat a thing in case Prince Amir showed up. But . . . what were *you* doing there?"

"I was . . ." Dread drips down Belle's spine. They saw her. Of course they saw her. She was too brash, too daring, too . . .

"Don't worry. The other two didn't— *Oooh. Ick!*" Marie gasps.

The fish heads have started to smell especially putrid, probably because Belle placed moldy cheese from the trash in between them to make the smell as rank as possible.

"What *is* that?" Marie groans at the sight of the fish, but Belle's not listening to her. She's listening to the sound of scurrying little feet within the walls, under the floor, along the pipes.

"Freedom," Belle whispers. The fish heads are a little trick she learned from the Rat King of the Midlands.

Rats burst up around them, swelling through the tiniest

cracks, seeming to materialize out of thin air, some even plopping down from the unlit fireplace, descending upon the fish heads.

Belle leaps onto the bed, pulling her feet to her chest as the rats surge over the floor.

"Hurry," Belle encourages Marie, fighting back goose bumps. "Tell your mother and sister to get out of the house."

Marie doesn't move. And Belle realizes that Marie hasn't screamed or flinched or fainted or joined her on the bed.

Instead, she's kneeling among the rats, beaming so wide, Belle can see the maple candy tucked against her back molars. She pats rat heads and strokes rat backs and tickles rat tails.

"Aren't you precious?" she coos. "I wish I could keep *all* of you!"

Belle gapes.

No. This isn't supposed to be happening.

What's *supposed* to happen is a mob of rats racing up the stairs, flooding the Steinems' town house. And in the evacuation and mayhem, Belle would have the time to find the locket and flee.

There is *not* supposed to be any rat-petting.

"You should go warn your mom and sister," Belle tries again. "The rats . . . They carry disease."

Marie picks one up and tucks it to her chest.

"So do people," she observes. "But we have to get you

all out of here before Mama sees you," she says to the rats, and whistles.

In a heartbeat, the rats stop. The room falls silent. Some rats even sit on their back legs, looking at Marie expectantly.

"Everyone needs to get out," Belle attempts. "Call a professional."

"What do professionals know?" Marie rolls her eyes, and Belle is even more baffled. Marie whistles again, and the rats click, swish their ropy tails, squint their beady eyes, and then swirl back into cracks and cubbies, climbing up the fireplace. The cellar is filled with the sounds of little rat nails clicking over stone tiles.

"Hurry," Marie says, scooping up the fish heads and plopping them back into the buckets. "What *were* you doing with these?"

"Family tradition," Belle mumbles.

"Do I hear *rats*?" The cellar door flies open as the last few rats scurry back into the walls and beneath the floors, their tails zipping away into nothingness.

Belle had thought Simone unnerving when she was calm, but she's terrifying when she's upset. Her eyes blaze, her cheeks flame, and Belle wouldn't be surprised if her hair transformed into living, hissing snakes.

"It was just one," Marie explains. "We got rid of it."

Belle frowns. It's not defeat. Not yet. She could still try this again.

But the way Simone's fiery gaze turns on her makes Belle think that she knows exactly what happened.

"What a close call," she says, her voice dangerously soft. "How very lucky you were. *Marie.*"

Marie leaps off the floor, straightening her back and looking somewhere between annoyed and nervous.

"Since you've been kind enough to help Belle with her little rat problem, you might consider devoting just as much energy to a bath?"

Marie shoots Belle an apologetic look and dashes back up the stairs.

"Well. Get to cooking, then," Simone commands Belle. "The royal family is coming to dinner."

The door slams shut behind her, and Belle tries to whistle for the rats like Marie had, knowing there's no use. Speaking to animals is a very rare talent, one that Belle unfortunately lacks.

And Simone's words sink in.

The royal family is coming to dinner.

Belle grips her apron in excitement.

After all this, Simone might have just bought Belle her way out.

9

Ella

THE CANDLE'S LIGHT IS WEAK, BUT IT SHOWS Ella just enough to race up a curving stone staircase toward what she hopes is the exit, stumbling a little as the knee above her glass leg sings out in pain.

Ella's not going to go from wasting away in Simone's cellar to wasting away in some slimy prison.

She bites the insides of her cheeks to keep her focus as the pain in her knee worsens. Her eyes burn. She hates that she has to have a glass leg in the first place. She hates that it's been hurting. She hates that her father had to go and die. She hates that Simone couldn't have had even one more drop of kindness. And she hates that life isn't like she dreamed it would be.

Finally, Ella reaches the main floor, where thick, dusty

curtains shroud all the windows, and ceilings vault up and disappear. Frozen shapes loom in the dark. Statues, Ella hopes. Really, really hopes. Each of her footsteps echoes like she's being followed. The hair on the back of her neck prickles.

The candle lights a wavering path forward, Ella's grip on it trembling, until she can make out the massive wooden doors of the entry. She dashes forward, hauling at the handles with all her strength.

And nothing happens.

They don't budge. They can't be shoved or yanked. She asks them to open, but they're apparently much smarter than the cell door. She throws her shoulder against them and kicks at them with her non-glass foot until she has to admit that they might be locked.

A key. That's it. Ella has to find a key. In her father's stories, plenty of people have to find plenty of keys. Thinking about his voice, as comforting as a hot cup of tea, helps calm her clattering teeth, her shaking hands, her frantic heart.

The problem with those stories is that people always seem to know where to look. The whole searching part goes by in a flash to get to the heroism and romance. Except now Ella is in a giant castle inhabited by creatures she doesn't want to imagine, and she doesn't even know where she should *start.*

So she begins with the nearest room, the darkness so thick she can nearly feel it. To keep her bravery, even while her fingers are trembling from fear, she thinks of Amir, of the stories she will have to tell him. Sure, they had parted on a terrible note. An awkward, terrible note, and she's not sure he'll ever want to speak to her again, but maybe he'll forgive her to hear about this: an enchanted castle, the fearsome beast of the woods made real.

This room smells just as bad as the dungeon. The floor is slick and spongy with damp, and the furniture looks either moth-eaten or mold-covered. There is not, as she hoped, a box full of loose keys that appear perfectly sized for a massive door.

Ella uses her small candle to light a three-armed candelabra, dusting off a spider. Even this casts little more than a pale, greasy glow and barely illuminates the room. Ella yanks open drawers in a bureau, sifting through random papers with the ink nearly faded, old ribbons, shards of what looks like a broken teacup.

No key.

"You prefer to test your luck?" A rough, rumbling voice growls, as hair-raising as fingernails scraping down a chalkboard.

Fear freezes Ella.

"You would have been safer in the dungeon."

The voice is so horrible that Ella wouldn't be surprised if the candle sputtered out, if bricks tumbled out of the walls. The voice clogs her blood and makes her dizzy with nerves.

Ella brandishes the candelabra in front of her. If only it

were a sword. If only she could wish hard enough to transform a candelabra into a sword.

The voice laughs, a sound like daggers clattering together.

"A liar, a thief, and a fool."

The figure prowls toward her as the candle's light falls on Ella's face, and she preferred the disembodied voice. Shadows seem to shroud it, but the candlelight gives Ella glimpses. Dark, shaggy fur. Long, yellowed claws. Fangs as long as Ella's hand. Eyes as green as poison glimmer with fury and hunger.

Ella tells herself to be brave, but she can't help shrinking back.

"You." The beast sounds genuinely surprised. Surprised, Ella figures, that the liar, thief, and fool is a twelve-year-old girl who's somehow gotten herself into this situation.

"Who are you?" Ella's voice trembles. She wishes she could squeeze her eyes shut and make this all go away. "What are you going to do with me?"

"Should I say?" The beast growls. "Or is it better not to know?"

Ella can't exactly see how big the beast is, but it seems somewhere between very, very large and very, very enormous. A horrific smell radiates from it.

"You can't keep me prisoner!" Ella cries.

"I already am."

"You haven't done a very good job," she spits.

The beast stills. For a moment, Ella thinks she might have cowed the beast with her cleverness.

But it's a very brief moment.

"You're bold for a thief," the voice growls. "But there are worse punishments than dungeons."

"I didn't even take your stupid clock." Ella jabs the candelabra in front of herself. At least, she didn't take it from the castle.

"Someone has to suffer for it," the beast says.

"Is that suffering being forced to smell your breath?" Ella parries.

A bad thing to say.

Ella has spent most of the last few years wondering if what she said was a bad thing to say. Usually it's not as disastrous as she expects.

But this *is*.

"I was considering showing you mercy." The beast's lips peel back, revealing more and more sharp, yellowed fangs. Its hot, rancid breath drifts over her. "But the world is luckier to have a girl like you locked away."

Ella might as well be listening to Simone. How many times had Simone promised kindness or mercy if only Ella hadn't done this or if Ella hadn't done that?

"You don't get to trap me here," Ella argues.

Gripping the candelabra, she dodges underneath the beast's arm and through the castle. Her knee hurts badly enough to give her a headache, but she doesn't stop.

Ella races toward the heavy doors. Still, they won't open, no matter how hard she shoves them. But only Henrik knows where she is, and, if the stories are true, then the castle is hidden by magic. No one but Henrik could ever find her.

Ella's going to have to rescue herself.

"Open," Ella threatens the doors in a low whisper, holding the candle's flickering flame up to the wood. "Or I'll set fire to you."

And either the doors take pity on her or the warning works, and they open just slightly, enough that Ella can squeeze through and out into the garden. She stumbles forward, her knees and palms grazing the sharp gravel. The candelabra falls and gutters out, but sunlight peeks behind the clouds.

The frost in the air claws at her skin as Ella glances down the path lined with pomegranate trees to the wall of thorns and the Dreamwood beyond. To freedom. Even without a glass leg, she wouldn't be able to outrun a beast that distance. And within the woods, there could be wolves. Or worse.

A horse. They had made it through the woods safely on horses. Ella can't think of anything she would like less than getting onto another one, except for being eaten by a beast with terrible breath.

Ella veers toward where she had remembered seeing stables, hobbling as the pain in her knee above her glass leg grows more intense. And yes—there are horses, to Ella's relief. Although they look . . . They don't exactly look like regular horses. Ella can't put her finger on it, other than that they look like . . . like they're made out of tin.

"I need your help." Ella's words tumble together as she reaches the horses, though without Henrik's help, she has no idea what to do next. How do you saddle a horse? How do you get on—do you just kind of jump onto its back, or . . . ?

"You let her *out*?" the beast roars, so loudly that it rattles the sides of the stable, and all the horses begin neighing frantically. Their eyes look—impossibly—like they're painted on. Their manes—impossibly—like they're made of ribbons.

"All of you. Get out of here." Ella limps down the row, unlatching each stall, feeling a little like a heroine. But most of the horses just stare at her like they know they can't outrun a beast, either.

Ella decides that they're wrong. Something needs to be said for looking at a terrifying thing and scowling back at it.

Even if right now Ella's stomach is flip-flopping and she doesn't dare peek behind her in case green eyes are glinting through the dark.

Unsure what else to do, she clumsily scrambles up the wall of the stall, half-crawling her way onto a chestnut pony's back. It also doesn't feel the way Henrik's pony did. This feels like sitting, well, on a horse made of tin.

Ella has enough to worry about without trying to figure out how that happened.

The tin horse whinnies in annoyance, but the beast lets out another roar, and the pony quiets, shivering.

"Run!" Ella braces for the wind in her hair, the horse pounding them toward freedom. "Go!"

But the pony just prances in place.

And . . . and how do you make a horse *go*? Henrik's pony had started trotting at his whistle. Ella had thought that was something they just . . . did.

"Run . . . *now*!" Ella commands.

The pony trots in place like it's annoyed at her.

"Go!" She orders, slapping her heels against its sides—it makes a dull *thunk*—and gritting her teeth at the pain in her left leg.

The pony flies out of the stable and over the grounds, and Ella steers him—

Except she's forgotten how that part goes, too.

Without reins, as the pony darts forward on stiff, unbending legs, Ella can't do anything but cling to its metallic neck, spitting as its ribbon mane flies into her mouth. The pony zigs and zags among the thorny bushes and the pomegranate trees, confused and scared.

The beast roars, a sound as massive as a lightning storm about to crash over a city. The pony bucks. Ella cries out as the sturdiness of the pony is replaced by nothing but air.

The last things Ella sees are the beast's poison-ivy eyes and its claws lurching toward her.

10

Belle

FOR THE ROYAL FAMILY, IT MUST BE GOLD.

Or, at least, what Simone claims to be gold leaf, just as she claims the garden pigeons are quails and the mealy pears lying in the dirt in the garden make the best tartlets.

Her hair frizzing around her face, Belle plucks and chops and roasts and sprinkles fake gold flakes, working alongside the neighbors' servants that Simone has hired for the evening. Even though the kitchen is a floor above the cellar, a rat occasionally pokes its head into the kitchen, sniffing at the smell of roasting pigeon until Belle commands it to go away.

The Steinem house is in a frenzy with preparations, and even Fiona and Marie are forced to make sure not a trace of dirt lingers on the floors for when the queen, the prince, and a few of their circle arrive. Marie sneaks into the cellar to complain about dusting and offer Belle chocolates, and Fiona sneaks down to stick her mouth in front of Belle's face to check if the peppermint leaves she's chewing are working.

"In case the prince kisses me," she titters.

"Ew," Marie says.

"There's nothing *ew* about kissing a prince," Fiona declares, twirling.

"I was talking about him having to kiss *you,*" Marie retorts, and Fiona storms out of the cellar.

Belle catches a frantic spark in Simone's eyes as she checks a nearly empty coin purse after paying the delivery boy for wine.

From conversations, Belle picks up bits and pieces: it's not common for the royal family to come (Belle could have guessed). But Ella's father was the royal librarian and the queen's personal friend, so she visits out of respect for his memory. And because Simone had gone to the castle every day for the past month with an invitation to dine.

It will just be the queen and Prince Amir—the king has made few public appearances since the princess left—but Belle and the neighbors' servants prepare a feast that could feed a dozen, more if no one gets seconds.

As soon as everything is done, Fiona and Marie ordered to their rooms, the servants standing at attention, and Belle wiping up the table in the cellar, Simone floats down the stairs. She's dressed like a queen on her coronation day, her red curls piled high and strung with imitation pearls. Her skin is so pale against the dark velvet and lace of her gown that she seems to glow.

But she's wearing a waterfall of fake rubies, not the locket.

Which means that the locket is likely somewhere within the house.

Simone kneels beside Belle, careful not to rumple her dress, and Belle is swept into the fumes of her sugarplum perfume.

"Not a word from you, understand?" she whispers.

Of course Belle understands. She's here to make it seem like the Steinems are fine, able to afford a servant and to send Ella "off to boarding school," as Simone decided the story shall be.

"I'll be here," Belle says, and Simone sucks in her cheeks, eyes narrowing, and Belle's scalp prickles.

"You're an awfully polite little thing," Simone declares, but before she can say anything more, trumpets blare overhead.

The royal family is here.

Simone flushes, and she dashes away as much as a lady can dash.

Once she's gone, Belle bolts into action, discarding Ella's old dress for the shirt and pants she had come in. Simone was right to be suspicious.

Voices and music drift down through the floors, the hired violinist playing with the intensity that only fear of

Simone can inspire. Wine will start to flow, and then dinner, and then more wine, and then dessert.

An hours-long affair, Belle suspects, which gives her ample time to find the locket. A plan that's much less chaotic than rats.

Belle stands on top of the bed and squeezes through the window.

The garden looks even sadder during sunset, the rosebushes all brambles and thorns, the fruit trees knotted and barren. The house's stone sides blush a daring pink as the last of the sunlight hits it.

Belle studies the house. She hasn't been allowed into Simone's room, but she's cleaned the girls', and she can guess which windows are Simone's. She's just not sure how to reach them, the stone smooth and no vines clambering up the house's walls.

She grunts in frustration. Belle has traveled from Reverie's darkest depths to its airiest heights, but suddenly, a second-floor window is unreachable.

Well. No matter. Belle kneels in the soil, searching for pale mushroom caps. If she can find a false panther mushroom, she can use its magic to burn holes into the house and etch out rudimentary handholds. She's relieved that Henrik hasn't popped up, but she misses him now, part of her wishing they could hunt for the locket together, imagining how he might perk up with the quest.

Belle plucks a mushroom, holding it up to see if it's a false panther or just a true blusher.

"What are you *doing*?"

Belle leaps up, dusting off her knees and glowering.

A boy crouches on a small rock. He seems to be about Belle's age, and his dark hair is messy, his skin olive-toned, his eyes like sea glass. When he sees her, he gasps, revealing a small gap between his front teeth. He looks somewhat familiar, but she's sure she's never seen him before in her life.

"Are you here to help Ella, too?" He fiddles with his coat, purple with gold buttons. It doesn't fit him properly—borrowed, Belle figures, or stolen. Perhaps he's a street urchin.

"I don't know Ella," she says. "My name's Belle."

The boy frowns with his whole body, his thick eyebrows inching together, his cheeks sucking in, and his foot starting to tap like he's trying to pound his surprise into the ground.

"Is she still in there?" the boy asks, peering down at the small window.

"Ella isn't here," Belle says. "I heard she . . . went to boarding school." It's the easiest explanation.

"There's *no way* Simone sent Ella to boarding school." His voice cracks. But before Belle can explain this whole mess, pitying him, a rusty voice creaks through the garden.

"Your Highness?" the guard calls. "You're not supposed to wander off."

The boy freezes. Belle stares at him.

"Your Highness?" she whispers. "You're . . ."

"Unfortunately."

He's not an urchin boy or a servant.

He's Crown Prince Amir of Miravale.

And he's about to ruin her attempt to get the locket.

"Over here!" the guards call, marching into the gardens in their purple-and-gold uniforms. "Prince Amir. You are not to go running off like that."

Amir casts a disgruntled look toward Belle. "As prince, it seems like I should get to decide where I go," he mutters.

The guards steer him toward the front of the house, and Belle tries to shift back into the shadows of a pear tree so she can continue her locket-hunting uninterrupted, but one of the guards frowns.

"And who are you?" His hand rests threateningly on his sword. "You realize this is a private garden, young lady."

"No. I mean, yes, I do, but it's not like that." The words tumble against each other like branches caught in river rapids. If she can just get the guards away before Simone notices her . . .

"There you are, my dear." Simone sweeps among the barren rosebushes, her smile sweet but her gray eyes flashing, and Belle's heart plummets. She grips Belle's arm in an iron clasp. "Sir Conrad, I don't believe you've had the pleasure of meeting my ward."

The guard blinks at Belle. He looks particularly relieved he didn't draw his sword.

"Ward?" Belle asks. Unease races through her veins.

Simone wasn't supposed to catch her outside. Simone wasn't supposed to suspect anything.

"Oh." Simone smiles. "That's an awfully impersonal word, isn't it? Dear Belle here lost her family recently. A *tragedy.* And since I have the means, I've taken her in." Simone's sharp nails dig into Belle's skin. "She's gone through so much, the poor dear."

"That's not true!" Belle declares.

Simone simpers, drawing Belle closer. Her perfume tonight is overpowering, and Belle has to keep from retching.

"It's *such* a pity," she says. "The little sweet still hasn't come to terms with losing her parents."

"That's terrible," Sir Conrad agrees. "I lost my parents when I was young, too."

And all Belle can do is glare, because if she says anything, Simone can write her off as being clouded with grief.

"It seems we've misplaced quite a few members of our party."

Belle has never heard the speaker's voice before, but she recognizes it instantly from the stories. The rhythmic accent. The stateliness of the tone.

Queen Milan strides into the clearing, her arms tucked before her, her fingers glimmering with rings. Her taffeta dress is modest and all black, as Belle has heard she's worn since the princess left the castle three years ago, sent to stay with some aunt by the sea. Like her son, her skin is olive, and her dark hair is pulled back. She is strikingly beautiful, and she looks tired, Belle thinks, but her smile is kind.

Belle is speechless. It's not that the queen is a *queen*—Belle has spent her childhood around dignitaries and royalty—but if anyone can get Simone to return her locket and free her, it's Queen Milan. Milan knows Henrik. They had met, years ago.

"Your Majesty," Simone says silkily. "Meet Belle."

Simone repeats what she's told the guard, adding even more tragic touches to Belle's made-up life, and when Belle opens her mouth to cut in, Simone bends toward her.

"How much is that little piece of junk worth to you?" Simone whispers, acting like she's brushing a piece of Belle's hair out of her face.

Belle stiffens. And stays silent.

It's too much of a gamble. Simone already has the queen's confidence. How could Belle, a stranger looking half wild after a day in the kitchen, convince her that Simone has spun nothing but lies?

"Lady Simone, I have always known you to be a woman of considerable elegance," the queen says. "But I hadn't known how far your compassion stretched."

It turns out Queen Milan is a terrible judge of character.

"Let's not let the meal get cold," Simone says. "Please, go back inside. I'll join you shortly."

"Ought Belle to dine with us?" the queen asks.

"She's exhausted," Simone says. "It's a greater kindness to let her go to bed." She gestures toward the front door. "Please, Your Majesty. Our cook has prepared the very finest quail in Miravale."

As the guard leads the queen back inside, Simone digs her fingers deeper into Belle's arm.

"Come, Belle," Simone says. "Let's get you to rest."

As soon as they're out of earshot of the queen, Simone grimaces. She drags Belle through the back door, but they don't go to the cellar.

"You should have run when you had the chance," she warns.

11

Ella

THE FIRST THING ELLA SMELLS ISN'T FISH.

She's expecting fish.

Fish is usually one of the first things that wakes her, a bucket of that morning's catch plopped in the cellar for her to deal with, sometimes a few of the bravest trout still flopping.

Someone coughs.

Ella hopes it isn't one of the fish.

She rolls over, away from the sound.

Another cough, slightly louder.

Ella claps her hands over her ears.

"*See.* I said she was still breathing." Ella shoots upward. It would be either very good or very bad if one of the fish suddenly became concerned about her.

But no one is there.

"Who said that?" Ella demands. "Where are you?"

Ella glances around, confused. She's in a grimy, gray, strangely damp bed in a grimy, gray, circular room that smells like decay. With a sinking heart, she knows: she's back in the beast's castle.

A weak fire sputters behind a grate, failing to warm her against the cold. Out the window the morning sky is touched with peach, but the wind bellows, rattling the panes.

"Um. No one," the voice says after a beat.

The voice is coming from the corner of the room, near a wardrobe. Ella's sure of it.

Untangling herself from the dirty sheets, Ella limp-lunges forward, her hand seizing upon something—small?

The small thing squirms and clamps down on Ella's fingers.

Teeth. It's definitely teeth, except they feel like they're made out of felt, and the bite does little more than tickle.

Still, the surprise is enough, and Ella drops the small thing to the ground, scrambling back.

A mouse stares at her, his pink nose twitching as he straightens a little green vest.

"That is *not* very polite," the mouse scolds.

"You can't talk!" Ella declares, her head spinning.

He's not a mouse. Not exactly. Where fur should be, there is felt. Instead of a nose, a tiny ball of yarn. His eyes, buttons, and his tail, twine.

"I," the toy mouse retorts, "can talk very well. Thank you very much."

She knows that voice.

"You're . . . you're Stanley," Ella says. The person—mouse, she supposes—that visited her in the dungeon.

"What were you expecting?" Stanley huffs. "You're fine, if you're wondering. Might just be a little sore for a few days. You got lucky. Not everyone gets that lucky."

"I've heard of people being luckier," Ella says snarkily.

But at least she's not in the beast's stomach.

"We didn't *think* you'd be lucky at all." A bird swoops from the top of a wardrobe to land beside Stanley. It's a strange bird, made entirely out of jewels, every feather the color of a gemstone: sapphire blue, amethyst purple, ruby red, an emerald green that makes Ella shiver with a memory of the beast's eyes.

"Who are you?" Ella demands.

"That's Citrine," Stanley says. "I'm Sir Stanley von Wensilus VonTrapp Hagenauer Halstatt the Third. As discussed."

Citrine makes a disgruntled chirp.

Birds made out of jewels. Mice made out of felt. Of course, Ella has heard stories of magical objects, caught glimpses of a few at the castle, but Miravale has strict laws on magic, and the greatest enchantments they had at home were self-writing quills and cups that kept coffee warm all day. It's one thing to see and another to witness.

If all this is possible, is there any such thing as *impossible*?

"*What* are you?" Ella clarifies.

Stanley hops closer, peering at her. "Oh. I'm sorry. Are you— Do you need glasses? I'm a mouse."

"I don't need glasses," Ella retorts. "Aren't you . . . felt?"

"And what does that have to do with anything?" Stanley asks.

"I was right." The jeweled bird flutters onto the top of the wardrobe. "You have the wrong girl."

"I'm wrong?" Ella bristles.

"Citrine, we talked about—" Stanley begins.

The castle shudders.

Citrine squawks. "You said she wouldn't find out you brought the girl up here! Wrong quite often today, aren't you?"

The castle shakes again.

With footsteps, Ella realizes.

Very, very big footsteps. So big, Ella *feels* them in her bones.

Citrine and Stanley exchange worried glances, and Ella realizes two things.

She's not supposed to be up here.

And the beast has found them.

12

Belle

SIMONE DRAGS BELLE UP A STAIRCASE AND through an intricately carved door.

Her room has a large wooden bed on one side, a three-mirrored vanity on the other. A fire blazes in the hearth. It's feverishly hot, twisting with an exaggerated smell of smoke and sugarplums. Belle was supposed to enter here *alone;* by now she was supposed to be thinking of the Revel, locket already in hand.

"So," Simone says, her words taut with anger. "This was your plan? Sneak out while I was distracted?"

Belle has a good sense for danger, mostly because Henrik doesn't. It's kept her safe while sailing across the Vallian Sea in a perilous storm, while clambering through the treetop fortresses of the Rat King. Now, here's a glimmer in Simone's eye that Belle doesn't like.

"You took my—" But before she can finish and decide if it's a bad idea to say anything at all, Simone hisses, "That fool of a queen thinks I rescued a tragic orphan girl from the streets. *Do you realize what that means?*"

She does. Unfortunately. Now Simone's going to work even harder to keep Belle here, to maintain the lie and the queen's respect.

"You can tell her an estranged uncle wrote for me," Belle hurries to help. "To explain why I'm gone."

Simone sinks upon a velvet stool before the vanity and pours herself a snifter of brandy. The dark liquid seems to writhe of its own accord. The fire crackles and spits.

Despite the makeup, the firelight on her face, the ornate gown, Simone looks like something has been yanked out of her. Her face seems gaunt, her eyes crypts.

"There's nothing left," she breathes, more to herself than Belle. "But if they were to see one of my girls as a match for the prince . . . If they were to understand that we are a good, respectable family . . ."

That's it? This hubbub is to secure a promise to engage Fiona to Prince Amir when they're of age? All Belle's efforts have so far failed, but even she can tell this is a terrible one.

Simone waves her hand toward the edge of the vanity. "Here you go. What you want so desperately."

A large jewelry box. It's cracked open and—there. On top of the jewels made out of paste and peeling gold: her mother's locket. Belle can feel it, like a soft breeze, like music so familiar, it seems to be pulled from her bones.

The shadow of danger remains, but Simone seems . . . thoughtful. Regretful.

"Maybe my father has something that can help," Belle tries again.

"It's rather gaudy, isn't it?" Simone ignores her, pulling out the locket. It spins lazily, the light bouncing off the chain. Belle's heart twists. "Come here, then."

Belle's father used to tell her stories of what lurked in the woods, the goblins and the robbers and the witches that boiled children in pots. As their caravan lurched throughout Reverie, he'd teach her how to get herself out of scrapes and protect herself from monsters.

No one told her that sometimes the worst beasts are the ones who invite queens to dinner.

Belle approaches Simone, each step feeling like she's treading upon knives. Her skin is tingling. There's magic about, and the locket has never made her skin tingle quite like this, like the feeling right when you're about to become sick.

"I saw you looking around when you first arrived." Simone's words drip icicles, even as she smiles. She rubs her fingers over the locket. "My furniture. My jewels. All our once-nice things. I gave up everything. Have given it up, time after time. To survive."

"Things can change," Belle rushes to say. She tries to take a step back, but Simone yanks at her wrist.

"But, you see, I do know when there's something of value," Simone continues. She tosses Belle's mother's locket into the jewelry box with disdain and a curled lip, rooting through the rest of the contents. "And I know the few things that are still worth quite a lot." She clamps a bracelet around Belle's wrist. "There. It serves you better than the locket did anyway."

It's like feeling a snake bite without realizing it's lunged; it's like discovering you've swum too far out to sea.

Belle tries to pull back. Too late, she understands what Simone has placed around her wrist.

Belle falls to the ground, crying out. Her arm tingles with heat, but it's the shock that rattles her core.

"You can't" is all she can manage.

"I can," Simone says. "It's dangerous for girls to think they're so clever. Some say it will even get them cursed. Really, darling. This is for your own good."

Belle feels dizzy, the room tilting like the edge of a cliff once did, before Belle and her father scrambled to safety, watching as rocks tumbled hundreds of feet into the desert below.

Around her wrist is a manacle of obedience, a cruel instrument created by a fairy several decades ago, compelling the wearer to do whatever the owner intended. Good rarely comes from a fairy object, but people always forget magic isn't something to be played with.

Simone smiles. "Be grateful I'm so kind."

Belle's fingers scrabble at the bracelet, trying to unlock it, but it remains stubbornly closed. She squeezes her hand into a fist and tries to yank it over her knuckles, but the iron seems to tighten. She's heard about these, of course, but has never seen one. They were most often used on princesses, to make them as obedient as the stories claimed they were.

Simone frowns, tapping her long crimson nails on the manacle. "Now. How do we see if this lives up to expectations?"

For once, Belle bites down on her tongue and doesn't explain something she could.

"You said your father trades magical objects. You know how this works, don't you?" Simone asks. "Tell me."

"The wearer has to do whatever the wielder commands." The words spit from Belle so fast, so involuntarily, that she barely realizes she's spoken. She grimaces as Simone smiles.

"What's the first command I should give you, then?"

Belle's fingers fly toward her lap, the manacle feels like it's pinching her, and her tongue betrays her once again: "To not let anyone know that I have the manacle."

"Don't let anyone know you have the manacle," Simone commands.

She sinks back and swirls her brandy.

"I'm not terrible," she says tightly. "If that's what you're thinking. I'm not some wicked witch who locks up little girls. But I have my daughters to think of, you see. I won't let them live the life I have."

Belle doesn't think she qualifies as a *little girl,* but she does want to point out that locking her up is exactly what Simone is doing.

Simone continues. "You will not contact your people. You will tell everyone that you chose to work for me, and you are so grateful for this opportunity, being the orphan you are. You will not do anything to harm my family. You will not steal your locket or tell anyone else about it. You will do whatever my daughters ask. You will not leave unless given explicit permission, and you will always come back."

Blood pounds in Belle's ears as the bracelet pinches her with each of Simone's commands, like it's listening. The words weave around her, a spider's web keeping Belle from the Revel of Spectacles and freedom.

"Have I forgotten anything?" Simone asks.

Yes.

"Yes," Belle says. She's forgotten many things, including to be very, very specific and to make Belle tell the truth. Which could help her get out. She just needs to make herself a loophole, something outlandish enough that Simone won't believe it possible but that Belle knows is possible indeed. "You said I wasn't allowed to leave the house without your permission. What if it's on fire?"

Simone's brow furrows. Belle wishes she had a manacle

of intuition so she could read the thoughts brewing in Simone's mind.

"Yes," Simone agrees. "You can leave if the house is on fire."

"What if there's a goblin attack?" Belle asks.

"Then the cellar might be the right place to be." Simone deliberates. "But yes. You may leave if there's a goblin attack."

"What if a prince asks me to leave?" It's a question of desperation. All she can think of are those princesses, forced into obedience, wooing kings for an attempt at freedom.

"A prince? For you?" Simone coughs out a laugh, choking slightly on the brandy.

Belle needs a *yes.*

"What if a prince . . . kisses me?"

This time Simone does spit out her brandy.

"If a *prince* kisses *you,* then you're welcome to take the bracelet off yourself."

Belle tries to look horrified at the impossibility. Except, she has a prince in mind who has a habit of befriending girls in cellars.

A kiss. Belle has never kissed anyone, but that's how so many of the most famous stories go. It can't be *that* hard to make it happen.

"Now go, then, straight to the cellar. Talk to no one," Simone commands. "I have a queen waiting."

AS SOON AS BELLE'S BACK IN THE CELLAR, THE drafty quiet a welcome relief from the perfumed heat of Simone's room, the gravity of her situation strikes her.

She can't break any of the manacle's rules. She can't steal the locket. She can't escape. She can't get to the Revel. She can't do anything unless Simone allows it.

This is bad. This is very, very bad.

If only she hadn't used the pirate's spyglass. If only she had sent her father a letter immediately when she had ended up in Simone's basement. If only—but you can't *if only* yourself out of a bad situation. You can only go forward or stay stuck.

Which is why Belle refuses to divert from her plan:

1) Steal the locket.
2) Escape (without breaking the manacle's rules).
3) Get to the Revel and win the competition.

All she needs is a prince. *The* prince.

She keeps herself busy as the plates clink upstairs, people chatter, the violinist leaps through waltzes. She looks obedient whenever Simone sticks her head in the cellar to check on her. And when Simone's gone, Belle yanks at the manacle. Tries to saw it off with a kitchen knife. Sticks her hand close to the fire, hoping the heat will make the metal expand. Bangs her wrist against the table in hopes of shattering it. But all she manages to do is narrowly miss nicking her skin, get uncomfortably hot from being so close to the flames, and make her wrist ache. She considers setting the house on fire but doesn't want to risk the locket getting destroyed. And she doesn't know where to get any goblins.

So. Plan Prince it is.

Once the violin has quieted, the prince in question has departed, Fiona has called for her hot milk with honey, and Belle has had no choice but to bring it, Belle sits against the bed in the cellar so she can hastily stuff the letter away in case someone enters and begins to write.

Dear Crown Prince Amir—

She crosses it out.

That's not right. But she doesn't know how Ella talks or thinks, let alone writes.

There's no time to waste second-guessing.

A—

I'm back. Come see me?

—E

Belle twists the manacle around her wrist. It'll have to do. Sure, it's a lie, but it's a necessary one. And once Ella's actually back here, they'll forget all about it.

She stands on top of the bed and cracks the window open.

"I'm not going outside." She makes a face at the manacle. "Don't worry."

Instead, she whistles the same tune she's heard the doves singing. Belle can't speak to birds, although she's heard the princess of Apfel can, but she can mimic them decently enough. They're morning birds, but it's late enough at night that technically, it's a very, very early morning.

A fluttering.

A small dove, its feathers fluffed up like it's irritated to have been woken, hops over to the window. It blinks its beady eyes at her, tilting its head.

"Here," Belle whispers, extending the note. "It's for Prince Amir."

The dove hops closer, cooing quietly.

"I need help," Belle explains quietly, holding up her wrist with the manacle for the bird to see. In the wild, doves are intelligent creatures and good friends of witches, but Belle isn't sure what a lifetime in the city might have done to this one. "Can you get this to him?"

Either out of sympathy for Belle or simply out of habit, the dove extends one leg, and Belle grins. It's hard to tie the letter to the bird's leg with one hand—the hand with the manacle simply won't lift up near the window—but soon the bird is airborne with its letter.

And all that stands between Belle and the Revel is a prince's kiss.

13

Ella

THE BEAST'S FOOTSTEPS RICOCHET AS THEY thunder closer, and closer, and closer.

Stanley grimaces. "Stay put," he commands Ella, like she was planning on delivering herself on a platter to the beast.

Stanley darts out the door, wrenching it shut behind him as the footsteps grow louder and louder, the paintings on the wall starting to shake, Ella's teeth chattering.

"No. No. No. Don't— It's so boring on this side of the castle. Surely you'd prefer to be somewhere else." Stanley's voice pitches up at least two octaves. The footsteps stop.

"You put her up *here*? What is *she* doing up *here*?" That terrible voice rips through the walls, spilling into the room, and Ella can imagine the tusks, the claws, the terrible green eyes.

"Am I going to be eaten?" Ella whispers to the bird.

Citrine stretches her bejeweled feathers. "That's my concern?"

"She's going to be here for a while, isn't she?" Stanley points out to the beast.

For a while? Ella wonders.

"She might as well have somewhere nice to rest!"

"The only nice thing she deserves is to be alive. For now."

"Well, then, this shouldn't bother you at all," Stanley quips, "because death might be a little nicer. There's nowhere *nice* to sleep in this entire place."

"She is a *prisoner*," the voice growls.

There's a pause. The temptation to open the door and see what's happening is so strong that Ella feels almost faint—has the voice eaten Stanley, for instance? And what will happen to her if Stanley's eaten?

"*She* is named *Ella.* And have you ever thought," Stanley says softly, "that maybe she could be the one we're waiting for?"

"No," the voice says. "*Her?* No. Of course not."

Ella bristles. *Of course?* There's no *of course.* Ella could be *someone.* They don't know.

"The curse . . . ," Stanley begins.

"*Do not mention the curse.*"

"But the clock . . ."

"The girl is nobody. Nothing."

A low growl. Then the beast's footsteps retreat.

The door opens just barely, and Stanley slips inside, fanning himself. He looks queasy.

"Well," he says. "You probably want breakfast."

"You really believe this?" Citrine asks. "You really think it's her?"

"I think it's a *possibility.*"

"Who's what possibility?" Ella demands.

"Breakfast!" Stanley cries again, vanishing out the door and reappearing soon after, pulling a large toy train. Each car bears golden platters with steam pirouetting above. It looks like it belongs in a king's court, not in this moldering castle. And the smell.

The smell.

It makes Ella's mouth water. It warms her bones and wipes away the fatigue. It smells so good, like the entire point of all this—an angry beast, sacrificing herself for Henrik—was to eat this meal.

Of course, it could be poisoned.

Ella doesn't spend too much time weighing her options. She doesn't want to be the girl who dies from enchanted toast, but the beast has had plenty of opportunities to kill her without this extra effort.

There's a steaming silver pot of hot cocoa, a plate of fluffy scones topped with clotted cream, soft-boiled eggs, and roasted pears. To her surprise, it's Miravalian food. She and her father would often take plates like these out to the palace's quiet Everlasting Garden and eat overlooking a pond bobbing with lily pads. Sometimes Amir would join them. In one of her father's occasional bouts of mischief, he told Amir that people who could stand on two lily pads would have luck for the rest of their lives, and when Amir splashed into the pond, she and Redmond laughed so hard, she couldn't breathe.

"There was *supposed* to be a plate of cheese," Citrine notes.

Stanley pats his stomach, looking guilty. "I don't know what you're talking about. And no one likes tattletales."

It's been so long since she's had something other than crusted oats, raw carrots, and fish that tastes a little bit too fishy that Ella doesn't stop until she's licked the cream from her fingers and the plates are free of crumbs, and her stomach aches, but she doesn't care. She could be poisoned, and she wouldn't care. She might just ask for another scone so she'd go down on a high note.

"How was it?" Stanley asks.

"Worth the hassle of getting it." Ella means it to be cutting, but it comes out as praise.

"Good. Great." Stanley glances toward the door, his nose twitching. "Now. Since you don't like to stay put, you can roam this wing, and only this wing. You'll be safe, as long as you remain where I say."

An entire wing. A hot, delicious breakfast. Ella prickles with suspicion.

"Why are you being so nice to me?" Ella asks. "Yesterday, I was in a *dungeon*."

Stanley coughs again, scratching his tail.

"Oh, *go on,*" Citrine trills. "She's going to figure it out eventually."

Ella doesn't like that word: "eventually."

"You're like us now," he mumbles.

"I'm—I'm a mouse?" Ella asks, quickly glancing at her hands. They're still human hands, as far as she can tell.

"You can't leave," Stanley says. "The doors won't open for you again, no matter how many candles you have. She commanded it."

She? The beast is a she?

"You're stuck here," Stanley continues softly. "Forever."

14

Belle

BELLE'S WOKEN BY SOMEONE SHRIEKING.

Sunlight gushes in through the open cellar window, and Belle shoves herself upright. It's late. Exhausted by the night before, she's slept in far past breakfast.

The cellar door cracks open, Marie's head jutting through.

"Mama just realized there's no coffee," Marie explains. "She's a bit frightening. She wants you to deal with it."

Belle stifles a groan as the manacle pinches her, an unnecessary reminder that it's in charge as her body hauls her out of bed even while she aches to keep lying under the covers.

"And breakfast," Marie whispers. "You don't want to forget breakfast."

Like she's a marionette being controlled by a puppeteer,

Belle hurries up to the kitchen and prepares the hot milk with honey, puts on the coffee, butters the biscuits, and slathers them with jam, faster than she ever has. The magic is impressive, she has to admit, if it weren't so annoying. At least there are worse commands than having to make breakfast.

Fiona is sprawled on a sofa in the sitting room when Belle enters, flipping through that morning's newspaper and tossing aside the pages that don't interest her, which seem to be most of them.

"Do you believe in true love?" Fiona gushes, grabbing one of the biscuits from Belle's platter and tearing into it. "Because Prince Amir definitely felt that about me."

"He felt *something*," Marie mutters, licking the jam off her biscuit.

Judging by Amir's reluctance to go to the dinner at all, Belle thinks that a dragon giving away its treasure is more likely than true love on Amir's part.

"What's that?" Fiona's gaze narrows on the manacle, thinly veiled jealousy in her gaze. "Where'd you get that?"

"It's my mother's," Belle says, compelled to answer but not tell the truth, hoping that will make it sound priceless. "It's a family heirloom."

Could it be this easy? Fiona will take the bracelet out of jealousy. Belle hungers to see Simone's face when she discovers Fiona scrubbing the floor with lye.

"A *family heirloom*?" Fiona wrinkles her nose, and Belle

winces at her error. "The prince won't be interested in someone wearing *family heirlooms.*"

Belle trudges back down to the cellar. There's still a chance to trick Fiona into wanting the bracelet. A family heirloom it could be, but perhaps her aunt was the Queen of Apfel or one of the star catchers from the Sunset Isles.

Belle's stomach rumbles in anticipation of the spare biscuit and jam she'd left. Simone's instructions hadn't said anything about keeping some food for herself, and the bracelet has, surprisingly, made her feel bolder. Simone must have expected despair and resignation, but as long as Belle seems to be obeying, there's plenty she can get away with.

Starting with a proper breakfast.

In the cellar, Belle is met with a squawk.

The dove is waiting for her on the table, pecking away at the biscuit, but Belle's already forgotten about food as the bird extends one leg. Her heart leaps.

She rips the note open.

E—

Meet me at the market.

A—

15

Ella

ELLA THOUGHT BEING TRAPPED FOREVER BY the beast of the woods would be frightening, or horrifying, or exhausting from running from different spooks. Gremlins, surely, would pop out of the fireplace, or poltergeists would drop writhing clumps of spiders on her head, or murderous redcaps would chase her around, cackling and wielding rusted axes.

Ella didn't anticipate being *bored.*

It's been an endless, toiling, mind-numbing, unnaturally *boring* . . . two days. Technically, one and a half. But, technically, it feels more like years.

The food is delivered sight unseen and is mostly different takes on rice with vegetables, no more kingly feasts. Stanley hasn't returned, Citrine has remained atop her cupboard (she had informed Ella that she was only interested in talking if Ella had royal lineage, or was, at the bare minimum, a local celebrity), the dress she'd borrowed from Henrik is stiff with mud and starting to smell—but Ella hasn't found a tap that runs water that isn't brown—and there is no sign of the beast.

The rooms within the wing she is permitted to explore are nearly as dull as Fiona's imagination. In fact, Ella would rather be listening to Fiona talk about how Amir was going to realize they were True Loves, something she never thought she'd wish. When Ella catches herself even missing the rare moments of sitting around the fire with the Steinems and gossiping about neighbors, Ella pinches her elbow to remind herself that she hopes their oats are filled with cockroaches.

The rooms are nothingness. No furniture. No paintings or mirrors. There are only layers of dust and the stench of rot and spiders in the corners and an unshakable chill. If this is to be her *forever*—

No. It can't be. It won't.

Ella gives escape her best efforts, but the doors out of the wing won't budge, not even to threats or insults. She's tried holding candles to them, just to check, but the flames are snuffed out before they can so much as touch the wood.

With nothing else to do, Ella returns to her map.

In the royal libraries, her father would plant her at his favorite table, the one underneath a stone arch from an ancient Elven civilization, and let her pore over maps that were cracked and faded with age. As the junior librarians drifted past like moths, Redmond would promise they would make their own maps. They'd venture across Reverie, to discover every corner of the land.

Ella adjusts how she's sitting to lessen the aching in her leg. It's so quiet that it almost feels like Ella's dreaming.

"This is all your fault," she mutters to no one and everyone, abandoning the map. She dusts her charcoal-covered fingers off on her skirt and nudges one of the windows open. A sharp wind helps sweep away the smell of wet fur and mold, but outside it's also drab and gray.

She glances down at the map. It's supposed to be the Miravalian Palace, although all it's managed to do is make her miss Amir and her father.

Everything that's happened must be somebody's fault, and Ella is desperate for someone to blame.

Before Ella was trapped in a beast's castle and before she was trapped by her stepmother in a cellar, there was a king who had convinced her father to tend to his library.

The king was the son of the Miravalian king before him and the king before him, and the long line of kings before him. But the queen came from the south and the east, a distant land of genies in bottles, jewels said to be as big as a fist, shifting sands that stole and sold your secrets.

People spoke highly of Queen Milan in public, as people always do publicly, but in private they gossiped. Because she was from far away and a land less known, they claimed she had treacherous loyalties and dangerous magic. They blamed her for everything: crop failures, unfortunate run-ins with fairies and bandits, when they drank too much wine and felt ill the next day, their unrequited love affairs.

It didn't matter that the rumors were untrue; people still believed them.

Queen Milan and Ella's father were good friends. Her father was also from far away. He'd come from the Far North, where glaciers creaked and moaned, where birds as big as fear roosted in icy peaks, where the sea seemed to vanish straight into the stars.

Amir and Ella grew up on the palace grounds and became fast friends. They hunted tadpoles and ghosts, watched the guards practice, tried on the crowns in the throne room. Amir snuck out of the castle, and Ella invented errands so they could wander around Grimm Park, the market, the royal zoo to see its chimera and griffins and one wyvern. At least, she and Amir *were* friends, until Amir went and ruined it.

The princess, on the other hand, was terrible. Ella's father relayed stories of her petty torments: worms in his meals and sneezing herbs in his coffee and hot pepper in his breakfast jam. Her father excused the princess's behavior with his usual gentleness, but Ella felt a steel-sharp fury.

The pranks grew worse. The princess would sneak into the library and research rooms, unleashing buckets of slugs onto the old texts, or holding up matches to the thin pages, or opening the windows so birds flew in and tore out chapters to use for nests.

Of course, there was no proof that it was the princess—although Ella knew. She *knew*—and eventually, the king could no longer turn a blind eye to the destroyed books and scrolls. Despite Queen Milan's efforts, Ella's father was dismissed.

Without her father at the royal library, the family's dire situation became apparent. Simone spent money freely, under the mistaken assumption that because Redmond knew the king, he was a wealthy man. He received many benefits working at a palace, but he donated much of his salary to increase research funding.

Then, newly married, newly concerned about money, he took a job at an orphanage, teaching the children to read. The Miravale orphanages were in poor shape, and disease often prowled through them. The people who worked there were used to it, needing nothing more than a day at home and hot broth when they became ill.

Perhaps because Ella's father was from the Far North, his body had never developed immunity to the Miravalian illnesses. Perhaps he was already falling ill. Perhaps, perhaps, perhaps.

As her father lay with the fever, Ella brought him hot water with peppermint leaves and calendula buds. She sat on the small chair near his bed as he told her stories of fairies who could speak to flowers and underground cities of gold, her imagination marching her away from the sick room to impossible, wonderful lands. Redmond grew thin, his entire body trembling when he coughed, but his blue eyes still sparkled, his stories still dazzled.

Ella shakes herself out of her memories and the bitter taste they leave. The princess, Amir's sister, vanished from court, gone to visit an aunt by the Eastern Sea. Of course a princess never faces a real punishment.

It was a long time ago, even though the reason behind the princess's disappearance plagued Amir, who could never settle for questions with half-built answers.

Through the window snow drifts and flurries, an endless expanse of dark gray clouds overhead. The flakes land on the gnarled pomegranate trees, the wall of thorns, the bushes, the—

Ella shivers harder.

The beast. It prowls about the gardens and around the frozen lake, snow clinging to its coat. It leaves large, misshapen footprints.

It's the first she's seen of the beast since her failed escape and the first she's seen of it in daylight. The head of a lion, the body of a bear, the tail of a wolf, the tusks of a wild boar, mashed together into a creature hideous, hunched, cruel.

Ella watches the beast, waiting for it to do something especially beastly, like mutter curses at baby birds, but instead, it's just—walking, with its head tilted down.

For a moment, Ella wonders what it might be like to be a beast, but then she swipes the thought away. All it takes to be a beast is to enjoy trapping people for eternity. If there were no beast, Ella could stride straight out of the castle.

But something isn't right. Something has changed.

Chills cascade down the back of Ella's neck. It's the sky. It's the air. The temperature plummets, even inside the castle.

Ella presses her hands against the window, staring outward. Is it magic at the gate, being triggered? Is there someone out there in the Dreamwood coming to rescue her? She feels a brief flicker of hope that it's Amir. Maybe he's found her.

As she watches, a new cloud gathers in the sky.

Only it's not a cloud. Ella peers closer. It's a mass of birds, swarming together. They form a black splotch against the gray-and-white landscape.

They're just birds, Ella tells herself, but the sight sends goose bumps up her arms.

Like they're being commanded, the birds dive in the shape of an arrowhead toward the beast. In a mass of feathers and screeches, they fall upon it, until there's no proof of a beast at all beneath the heaving, cawing mass.

Ella leans forward, biting her lip so hard, she tastes copper.

The beast roars. Except this time, it's not a cry of anger and fury; it's a howl of pain. And though the beast has been terrible, it is still a creature, and it doesn't deserve whatever is happening to it now.

Ella yanks the window open and shouts at the birds, "Leave it *alone*!"

She waves her arms, yells, digs in her pocket for the food she's stashed, tossing a few rolls at them. It doesn't make any difference.

"Leave it alone!" Ella cries. "What has it ever done to you?"

Probably a lot, Ella thinks, enough to justify an attack. And she isn't entirely sure why she's defending the beast at all. But she yells again, "Just . . . Just *go*!"

The birds have become their own type of beast, and through gaps in the massive cyclone, Ella catches glimpses.

The beast has fallen, lying still on the ground.

16

Belle

A DAY HAS PASSED SINCE PRINCE AMIR'S visit, and Fiona has yet to find another topic of conversation. Belle thinks that each detail has already been picked apart sufficiently, but Fiona isn't satisfied.

"You wouldn't understand what it means to pine for a prince who's pining for you," she declares for the hundred and seventh time that morning, apparently judging Belle interested because Simone's orders and the manacle compel her to dust the sitting room. "We spoke for *at least* an hour at dinner."

"He yawned through most of it," Marie points out, absently tinkering with the harpsichord. Belle catches her eye, and they both grin.

"He was *laughing*." Fiona hurls a pillow at Marie, lighting up pink to the tips of her ears. "You couldn't possibly understand true love."

"If he kissed you, would he turn into a toad?" Marie retorts, and Fiona shrieks.

Belle's barely listening, busy plotting how *she's* going to kiss a prince. She's been obedient, getting a head start on the chores before Simone comes downstairs for the day. All the chores except making a pot of coffee.

There's the sharp clip-clop of high heels, the stench of lemon smoke as Simone enters the sitting room. She's still in her robe, though her face is already painted with makeup, like it is every morning, ready to receive the queen even at this hour.

"*Where* is the coffee?" she asks, her gaze narrowing. "Make me some. *Marie*. Please stop rattling around on that blasted instrument."

Marie drops her hands to her lap, glowering.

"You're all out of coffee," Belle says, as politely as she can.

It's not a lie. That morning she dumped the bag of beans into the sewers, and they've long floated down to the street's dung heap. Not even the bracelet's magic could think digging through *that* to boil a pot of coffee is being obedient.

Simone heaves a heavy sigh. "The *burden* of my life," she declares.

"Oh, it simply isn't fair, Mother!" Fiona cries with such

forcefulness that Belle thinks she should consider a career in the theater. "Once I'm the princess, you'll never go a day without coffee."

"What a doll you are, dearest." Simone rummages through a side table, digging out a scrap of paper and a coin purse. She doles out a few silver coins, wincing as she weighs the purse, scribbles a grocery list, and passes them both to Belle. "Go to the market, then. You might as well be useful while you're there, but make haste. I don't have all day."

Belle tries not to grin. "Of course," she says. That worked out better than she had hoped. She imagines how proud her mother would be, how she might say the two of them are so alike in their cleverness.

"Can I come?" Marie perks up.

"Take Marie to the market with you," Simone commands.

Belle's enthusiasm clunks. Marie can't come. None of the Steinems can know that she's meeting a prince. Simone can't find out about her plot to escape.

But Simone plunks a sun hat on Marie's head and flicks her fingers toward the door.

"Off to the market with you, then," she says. "And, Marie, mind the hat. A sunburn will make you look common."

BELLE AND MARIE NAVIGATE CARRIAGES AND horses bustling along the cobblestoned avenues, flanked on all sides by Miravale's light-pink stone buildings. Everything is draped with purple and gold banners announcing the Revel of Spectacles.

Belle reads them greedily, as if absorbing everything about the Revel will make her participation even more possible. Marie, clad in a gingham dress with yellow lace, is overjoyed. She skips along the street and tosses her sun hat behind a bush, wringing out a promise from Belle to help her remember which one.

"What would Mama say if I entered the Revel's competition, do you think?" Marie muses.

"She'd say it's not ladylike to be awake at that hour." The Revel's competition always occurs close to midnight, a tradition Belle suspects is mainly due to the dramatic effect.

"I probably wouldn't be much good at it," Marie says sadly. "But I'd ask the royal family to let me study music in Coralon. What would you— *Oh.*"

Despite the manacle, there is nothing like Miravale's market to lift Belle's spirits.

Candy cane–canopied stands; piles of colorful fruit; glassy-eyed fish on ice; chocolatiers with trays of candies that promise to make you fly or make your enemy's tongue fall out, though Belle is sure they won't do more than make you dizzy; toymakers with windup dragons and tin soldiers that march along a table. All in Miravale's center square, with the cathedral on one side, and countless banks, taverns, inns, and boutiques lining the edges.

Neatly trimmed rosebushes separate the sidewalk from the streets. Outside the Garden House, Miravale's nicest inn, they're pruned into the shape of dancers midleap.

Marie gawks and points at everything, and Belle's own curiosity runs rampant even as her heart aches. It's strange here, without her father and his boisterous laugh. She wonders where he is, where his journey to find her has taken him.

High above an alley a woman shakes out laundry from a balcony. Street urchins dart around selling newspapers, and travelers from throughout Reverie sing their different languages.

Belle's gaze rakes through the crowd, but there's no sign of a prince. Or a prince pretending not to be a prince.

"Ella never lets me come to the market with her," Marie

confesses as they walk. "And it's so boring in that house, I could *scream.*"

"Not as boring as being turned into a crane fly," Belle says, remembering a particularly nasty situation with a cursed goblet she and her father once encountered.

"If Fiona were a crane fly," Marie muses, "that would be an improvement."

Belle and Marie both snicker as they dodge merchants weighing swordfish fillets and mutton shoulders. Belle's surprised by how nice it is having Marie with her. The girls in her village found Belle strange for wanting to talk about magic or her travels, and while Belle had always told herself that you don't want friends who don't understand you, the sting never softened.

But Belle needs to focus on her mission.

There's still no prince.

"Look at that!" Marie declares, pointing at a farmer's giant pumpkin, "And that!" gesturing at a man painting people's portraits for the price of a daydream. "What do we do first? Do we—there's that! Or—look! Over there! Or that?" She points toward a cart where a small puppet show is being set up next to a man selling flavored ice.

"We find coffee. And carrots." Belle glances at the list. She needs to do just enough to keep the bracelet content, and hopefully something as mundane as carrots will shake Marie so she can look for Amir alone.

"Or we couldn't," Marie suggests. She kneels by a cardboard box. Tiny orange kittens scrabble inside.

"You need . . . new ribbons." Belle consults the list. "For your hair."

"Oh, do I?" Marie rolls her eyes, tugging at her curls, which have already sprung free of her current ribbons. "Will you come with me?"

"I'll get the coffee," Belle says. "Meet you here?"

"And then the show?" Marie asks.

"Sure," Belle agrees.

Marie trots away, and Belle dashes to a man with hefty burlap sacks behind his stall, scooping coffee beans into little paper bags.

Belle purchases coffee and carrots and bread, trout and apricots, keeping her eye out for a boy with dark hair and green eyes. But it's hard, with the bracelet tugging her this way and that. Whenever she wants to pause and look around for Amir, the bracelet makes her follow Simone's list.

At every outdoor café, around every vendor's tent, people gossip about what their royal favor would be, most people eventually confessing they won't be competing. They mention trolls, angry skeletons, misfired spells, scheming fellow competitors. Henrik, apparently, isn't the only one who judges it a bit dangerous, which just means less competition for Belle.

Soon she's gotten everything beyond Marie's hair ribbons, and there's nothing the bracelet can make her do as she waits for Marie. Belle branches down a side street. More than a few people are selling potions that will make you "extra strong" for the Revel, though Belle is positive they're just ink and rancid fish-liver oil.

She pauses near cages full of tiny pixies, snoozing in the midday heat. The vendor is selling them for three gold coins each, a fair price, since some pixies can hear secrets whispered half a world away, but an exorbitant sum when Belle is confident they're pygmy garden gnomes with wings taped onto their backs.

"Psst. You."

Belle glances around. The side street is still busy, but no one's looking at her.

"Yeah. *You.* Not Ella."

A hand lurches out from behind a barrel of watermelons, and green eyes blink at her from the shadows.

This time, he's wearing a newsboy cap and an oversized gray shirt, but there's no mistaking Amir. He has the same fizzing energy, the same nose with the slight bump on the bridge, the same shaggy dark hair poking out from beneath the cap.

Belle grins, relief sweeping through her. She hadn't realized how concerned she'd been that Amir wouldn't show up, that somehow they'd miss each other.

"Where's Ella?" He keeps looking over her shoulders.

"She's not here," Belle confesses.

Amir narrows his eyes, though they spark with hope.

"Where is she, then?"

"I . . . don't know" is all Belle can manage because

revealing where Ella is would uncover certain questions about where Belle is from, and then how she got here, and the manacle is not interested in any of those conversations.

"She's not— You don't— So, what? You're just like the rest of them, trying to get my attention?" His attitude turns icy as quickly as a gate falls into place. He spins on his heel, and Belle bolts after him.

"Wait!" She jogs by his side, catching his sleeve. "Please."

Belle's mouth tries to work, her tongue tries to form words, but the bracelet is as annoying as ever.

Amir huffs and starts walking again.

"You can't use me to win the competition," he spits. "And I'm not going to dance with you at the Revel, or whatever you want."

"Please. I don't want a dance." Belle grabs him again, and a woman stumbles into them, frowning. Belle coughs out an apology, hoping the woman won't study Amir too closely. "I want to help you. Help you find Ella."

She's thought about this carefully. To make a prince kiss you, he must at least tolerate you, and to get people to tolerate you, you help them out.

Amir frowns, digging his hands into his pockets. "Who are you?"

That's a complicated question.

"I . . . work for Simone," Belle says, only the manacle stopping her from rolling her eyes. "It's a long story."

"Why should I trust you?"

Belle glances around, just to make sure Marie hasn't popped up. No gingham, no red hair, no Marie.

"Because I'm good at finding lost things," Belle protests. Not her own locket, but that's another matter.

Amir narrows his eyes. "You lied to me once," he reminds her. "With the letter."

Belle's thirsty and her feet ache and she thought this would be a bit easier than it has been. She's offering to do something *nice.*

"Are you that stubborn?" she demands. There's something about being reliant on a prince that makes it impossible for her to control her frustration.

"Excuse me?" He stops short.

"Listen," she says. "I don't think Ella's at boarding school, either. And I want to help you find her."

All you need is one kiss, and the bracelet is off, she reminds herself.

"You think Ella . . ." Amir's brow furrows. "This is so strange. And . . . who *are* you?"

"Belle," she says, relieved that Simone hasn't issued a command about that. "Villeneuve. Of Villeneuve Trading."

"Oh. I've heard of you." Impossibly, Amir grins. "Yeah. Your dad gave me and my sister toys when we were younger." His bushy eyebrows jump, like his thoughts are racing across his face. "Your dad's kind of a weird guy, too."

"You have to be a little weird when you work with so much magic," Belle admits.

Amir considers this, sucking in his cheeks. "And what do you get out of it?"

"I can't tell you that." The manacle won't let her say more. Belle feels a little bad about keeping the truth from him, but she'll do him a favor. And he'll get her free.

"Okay, Villeneuve. Let's help each other." He juts out his hand, and she takes it quickly, before he can change his mind. They shake, and Belle tries not to think about how surprisingly warm and calloused Amir's hand is. She's *only* thinking about its impact on the Revel, she scolds herself. "The thing is, it's weird that both Ella and my sister ended up gone. I think something happened to—"

Someone gasps.

In a cloud of riotous red curls and gingham, Marie stares straight at them, her mouth wide.

"Belle," she gasps. "What are you doing with the *prince*?"

17

Ella

ELLA DASHES THROUGH THE CASTLE TO reach the beast and the swarm of birds. She hurtles down the stone stairs, and this time nothing stands in her way, every door swings open, and the pain in her knee is an afterthought.

She moves too quickly through the garden to savor her first time being outside since her botched escape, too quickly to think about the fact that she could just keep going, straight into the Dreamwood and far away.

She moves too quickly to think through why this is a terrible idea.

Ella throws herself among the birds, crying out at the peck of beak, the slash of wing. It's a whirlwind of feathers and talons and screeches, and Ella can feel more than she can see, wincing as daggerlike talons cut through her sleeves.

"Stop! Stop! Go away!" she shouts, flapping her arms uselessly and trying to stumble her way through the winged currents toward the beast. A falcon screams, barreling toward her face, and Ella gasps, dropping to her knees in the snow, ducking her head down to protect her eyes and covering her ears.

She doesn't know which way is out. She's not sure which way is forward. All she knows is that it must *stop.*

"Go. Away!" Ella bellows again.

Despite Ella being completely and utterly sure that it won't—it works.

As one, the birds soar upward, the mass splintering apart into doves, sparrows, ravens, owls, and goldfinches that flutter away.

The snow drifts lazily and quietly. It looks like a peaceful winter day except for the hulking beast curled in the snow.

Ignoring the bite of damp and cold, Ella crawls toward it. The beast is hurt. The fur is matted, and there are dark splotches that Ella thinks must be blood. Ella prickles with horror and guilt. It's almost like the birds had heard her anger at the beast, her thoughts of freedom. Like she made this happen. But that's impossible.

"Um. Hi." Ella touches the beast's shoulder lightly. The beast doesn't move. "Are you okay?"

"Leave me," the beast growls, but its voice is muffled and

weak. Snow tumbles around them, and Ella's borrowed cotton dress does little to keep her warm.

"You're bleeding," Ella says softly, teeth chattering as she studies the beast. Ever since her father died, she's had to deal with Fiona's and Marie's scrapes and cuts, washing and bandaging their wounds, even when they were so shallow, they were hardly worth mentioning. But Fiona has a flair for the dramatic.

"Go away," the beast whispers. There's a snuffling sound, and Ella, to her surprise and surprising pity, realizes the beast is crying. Beasts aren't supposed to cry.

But this one definitely is. And there's even a little bit of snot.

"Leave me," the beast moans, and Ella's heart squirms. The beast has been cruel to her, sentencing her to a life spent locked away from the world. But now—

If Simone were in Ella's shoes, she would see this as an opportunity. *Make your own fate* and all that.

But Redmond would remind Ella that we get to choose to take a situation and make things worse, or we can try to make things good. And though goodness is harder, it grows.

Ella plants her hands on her hips and glances toward the path lined with pomegranate trees. And freedom. She looks at the gloomy castle looming behind her.

The beast locked her up, shoved her into a dungeon, threatened her, and had terrible breath.

But no one has come for the beast except Ella. Could it

be that the beast is just as alone as she is? Could she turn her back on such a creature?

"Come *on,* then, um, you." Ella juts out her hand, wondering if this is the part when she gets eaten. The beast ignores her. "I won't bite."

"Neesa," the beast grunts.

"What?" Ella frowns. Is that a spell, or warning, or secret language?

"My name . . . Before, my name was . . . Neesa."

"Before?" Ella asks, but the beast has stopped responding, groaning in the snow.

Neesa.

It's only a name, but in an instant the beast doesn't seem quite so monstrous.

"Neesa," Ella says. "Come *on.* It's freezing."

It takes a moment. Then, sighing, the beast grabs Ella's hand.

Its—her?—paw is the size of a dinner plate, her claws as long as Ella's fingers, but her touch is almost gentle as Ella helps her up.

Ella helps the beast up, swallowing a gag at the rancid smell. Maybe it's not easy to get clean when you're a beast.

You've dealt with worse, she reminds herself. *Remember the time Marie left cherry tartlets under her bed for so long that they got maggots? The time you had to pop all the pimples on Fiona's back before she went to a party for the ambassador of Apfel?*

Slowly, with Ella supporting the beast's weight, they

lumber through the gardens, past a few sparrows and goldfinches roosting in the pomegranate trees.

"Be nice," Ella instructs them, and the birds cock their heads and fluff their wings and trill little tunes.

When they reach the front hallway, Ella pauses but doesn't release the beast.

"What are you doing?" the beast huffs.

"Where's your room?" Ella asks.

"You don't get to know that," the beast growls.

She pushes away from Ella and tries to walk, but she stumbles, yelping as she collides with the stone tiles.

"I'm *helping,*" Ella says sharply, reaching for the beast again. "But if this is how you're going to act, maybe I should have left you out there."

Reluctantly, the beast lets herself be led once more. It seems impossible that Ella, as small as she is, as glass-legged as she is, should manage to help a beast so large and terrible up a flight of stairs and down seemingly endless hallways. Maybe it's magic. Or maybe it's just adrenaline.

Ella is starting to shake from the effort of supporting the beast by the time they reach her quarters, hobbling straight into the bathroom. It's larger than most rooms Ella has been in, with a massive sunken tub in the center and lamps that might have been pretty once but are now shrouded with cobwebs. The dust in here is so thick, it nearly hangs like curtains.

The beast slumps against a wall, her breathing heavy.

Ella turns the tap on, rusty water spitting and sputtering out, and she frowns at it until it begins to gush, like she's intimidated it into behaving.

"What is going *on*?"

Stanley rushes into the bathroom, his mouth wide and his little green vest askew.

"You *rogue*!" Stanley spins on Ella, taking in the beast, fur matted with wounds and dirt. "How could you? Back to the dungeons with you!"

"Me?" Ella snaps, shocked. "How dare you!"

She could have just walked away, abandoned the castle and the beast, but instead, she did the *right* thing.

"It wasn't her." The beast's voice is small and weak, nearly a mewl. "She saved me."

"From *what*?" Stanley's head pivots back and forth between them.

"From the *birds*." Ella's still bristling.

"The birds aren't supposed to attack!" Stanley says.

"*Supposed to* didn't seem to stop them," Ella snipes back.

The beast groans and slides farther down the wall, and Stanley hurries over to her, touching his tiny paws to the beast's fearsome ones.

"Go," Stanley commands, hurrying Ella out of the bathroom and slamming the door behind her.

Ella means to dash back to her room, but her legs betray her, and she sinks down onto the edge of a massive, scallop-shaped bed covered with fur and feathers that have seeped out of ruined pillows.

She's shaking from exhaustion and shock, and the scratches from the birds are starting to hurt, and it takes her a moment to realize that this room is possibly in a worse state than her own.

It's covered in a thick layer of grime that makes it feel like the walls are pressing in. In one corner little red toadstools are even poking through the floors, and Ella is sure she catches a cockroach scurrying out of view. Anyone waking up in a room like this would feel beastly, tusks or not.

Ella's expecting to feel fury, the cold seeds of revenge, but instead, she feels . . . concern. It's a terrible thing to be alone, aside from a toy mouse.

Ella needs to do something, and this is something.

There's nothing to clean with, so Ella rips off the bottom part of her dress, which isn't exactly clean, either, and wipes down a little table and the chairs. She beats away the worst of the cobwebs and scrubs away the soot on the wall left by the candles. She's not sure what to do about the mushrooms, but she can at least flap open the waterlogged books to help them dry.

It's not *intentional* snooping, but—there it is. On the bedside table. The clock, painted roses climbing up its sides. The start of this whole mess.

The time is wrong. The hands are past eleven, almost like they were at Henrik's, and they barely move at all. Maybe there's something wrong with the wiring.

Ella reaches forward, but from the bathroom the beast groans, and Ella flinches, scurrying back to her room.

Briefly, she stops at the front doors, which are still cracked open. But it's getting late, and soon it will be dark. At night the waiting Dreamwood seems more dangerous than a wounded beast.

Aching and confused, Ella collapses on her own damp, dank bed and her letter-thin pillow, and tumbles into a deep sleep.

SHE'S NOT SURE IF SHE WAKES UP FROM STANLEY clearing his throat next to her ear or because, for the first time since arriving at this castle, she's warm.

"Miss. Miss. Miss Ella," Stanley whispers. "It's Stanley. Sir Stanley von Wensilus VonTrapp Hagenauer Halstatt the Third."

A proper fire crackles in the hearth, her skin shifts against clean sheets, and her head is propped up by numerous fluffy pillows. Ella, it seems, is now the dirtiest thing in the bed.

"What's going on?" Ella scrambles up, wincing a little. Her left knee is starting to throb again.

Citrine perches on top of the wardrobe, staring at Ella with her unreadable jeweled face. "That was a very kind thing you did," she says.

"You did this?" Ella gestures at the room.

Citrine flutters her wings. "The castle did," she says,

like a castle showing gratitude is a perfectly normal phenomenon.

"For you, miss." Stanley hops over to the table by the fireplace, set with bandages, a small tub of ointment, clean blue pajamas, and a clean blue cotton dress. "The ointment's to avoid infection."

His little green vest is wet, like he's come straight from helping the beast. Ella pushes herself out of bed. It's dark outside, night curling through the windows, and Ella's stomach aches with hunger. She changes quickly.

"Is the beast alive?" Ella remembers. "Neesa?"

The birds left a few scratches, and she unscrews the ointment Stanley brought, rubbing it onto the cuts. It stings for a moment.

"She told you her . . . ?" Stanley's yarn nose twitches. "She'll be fine. She's recovering."

"Why would birds attack a beast?" Ella asks. "And why did the castle clean—*how* did a castle clean my room?"

Stanley fiddles with the buttons on his vest, clearing his throat, until finally Citrine lets out an irritated squawk.

"Because we're under a terrible curse," Stanley says. "And I think you're here to break it."

18

Ella

"ONCE UPON A TIME," STANLEY BEGINS, which makes Ella's mouth fill with a bittersweet taste because it reminds her of her father.

Once upon a time, Stanley explains, there was a girl who was forced to spend her days learning how to sew—she hated to sew—and how to curtsy, even though she didn't want to spend her life with her eyes toward the ground. She was never allowed to speak her mind, never allowed to walk outside of her garden, never allowed to laugh too loudly because her parents were afraid a fairy might hear and curse her.

As Stanley speaks, Ella sees a girl not unlike herself, forced to listen to everyone else without anyone ever listening to her. Maybe she had to sweep cinders, too.

She wished for freedom, she wished to be anyone but

herself, and one day, someone heard that wish. A wicked fairy came down and cursed the girl to grow larger and larger, fur sprouting from her skin, teeth misshaping into tusks, as terrible as any monster that was ever imagined. Her own family became terrified of her, forcing her to live in an abandoned castle deep in the woods, where the curse spread, twisting the castle into a state of dismay. The stuff of nightmares.

And, okay, yes. Maybe the girl hadn't always been Good with a capital *G*. Maybe sometimes she misbehaved. But can you blame her?

"No," Ella whispers, thinking of the times she switched the sugar for salt before Simone's morning coffee, or sprinkled ashes from the fire into Simone's night cream. Because sometimes the rules for being a good girl seem like they're made up by someone who cares about their happiness more than yours.

But the curse did not leave the girl lonely. It had turned her childhood belongings—Stanley points to himself—and some of her favorite trinkets brought to her by visitors—like Citrine and the tin horses—into real creatures to keep her company.

Neesa, the beast, just an ordinary girl? How does that happen? What was she *before*? A milkmaid or a merchant's daughter, an opera singer in training or a fledgling ore collector?

All fairy curses have rules, ways to be broken, Stanley continues, and this fairy left them with a riddle: *The curse could be broken by a thief who had stolen nothing.*

"That's why you think I'm the one to break it," Ella realizes. The clock. *Technically,* she stole the clock from Henrik, though Stanley doesn't know that. But was it stealing if, *technically,* she ended up returning it to its rightful owner?

"Fairy nonsense," Citrine observes.

Curses are a nasty business, Ella's father had told her. People who get caught up in curses can suffer fates just as bad, even if the curse wasn't meant for them. Ella could be risking her own life for a beast's.

For a girl's. A girl who is trapped, just like Ella.

"It's not just any clock," Stanley says. "The fairy gave it to us. It's counting down to the end of Miss Neesa's twelfth year. When the hour hand reaches midnight . . . the clock will stop. The curse can never be broken."

"And then?" Ella asks.

"Miss Neesa will stay a beast forever."

Forever.

An eternity in a beast's body. Without friends or family—

Well. Without human friends or family.

"The hand was past eleven," Ella realizes. "When's the bea— Neesa's birthday?"

"In ten days' time," Stanley says softly.

Ten days. They only have ten days to break a curse?

Ella calculates. That's the same day as the Revel's competition. Amir had said that he wanted Ella there. *I'll make you my champion,* he joked, even though Ella wanted to be her own champion before she was anyone else's.

"How?" Ella asks. "How do you think I'm actually supposed to *break* it?"

Stanley plays with his vest's buttons. "The fairy didn't get into all that," he admits. "But it can't be *that* hard, can it?"

That's optimistic of him, Ella thinks, considering they haven't managed to do it yet. And very optimistic that he thinks Ella's the answer. The only thing Ella's managed to break recently was one of Simone's vases, and that was intentional.

Curses are too dangerous to get in the middle of. Ella may feel bad for the beast, may understand her better than she wants to, but Ella has a *future.* She's going to have *adventures.* She can't risk being cursed by a fairy into a dung beetle.

"I'm sorry," Ella says softly, curling back into her bed. "You have the wrong girl."

19

Belle

BELLE POURS A THIN STREAM OF COFFEE into Simone's cup. Fiona glumly pokes at her chicken—no letter or word from Amir since the dinner. But Fiona *knows* that Amir felt the same connection she did, which she has announced multiple times during lunch already.

"Sugar?" Belle asks, extending the sugar bowl. Simone, scanning that day's society paper, doesn't even glance at her.

Marie waltzes into the room.

"Mama," she announces. "I need to go to the market."

Simone sets down the paper, arching an eyebrow. "You were at the market yesterday."

Marie doesn't meet Belle's eyes.

"I want to go back for the puppet show," Marie says cheerfully, even though she tugs at her skirt, her eyes a little bright with nerves. "You made us go home too soon last time."

"Let her go," Fiona sighs. "If she's home, she'll just play that horrid thing and bother me."

"It's a *harpsichord*," Marie retorts. "Maybe if you knew how to play one, princes would write you back."

"MOTHER!" Fiona screeches.

"Fine." Simone takes a sip of her coffee. "Belle. Take her to the market."

The manacle pinches her. Belle hides a smile. For once, everything is going just as it should.

20

Ella

THE BOAT ROCKS.

The boat—

There isn't supposed to be a boat.

Ella sits straight up, her heart hammering. This is—no—*no*. Ella gasps, feeling dizzy.

She's in a little rowboat, in her pajamas, and as snowflakes whisper around her, the winter wind claws at her.

And all around, there's water.

And within the water is something big enough to knock against the boat and make it sway.

This is—no.

No.

Ella can't swim. She—no. Whatever this is, it can't be

happening. Curses were enough. Beasts were enough. Not water. Not drowning.

Across the lake, a distance that could be as great as the world, the beast's—Neesa's—castle. And on the shore, Neesa.

The beast. Only a beast would come up with an idea like this.

"We couldn't get any sharks!" Stanley calls, waving. "But we managed to get some very large goldfish! I hope that works?"

Goldfish? A large orange shape drifts through the water. But it might as well be a shark, because the issue remains: Ella can't swim.

"What do you want?" Ella cries desperately, not too proud to beg anymore. She can't swim. Do goldfish eat you if they're hungry enough? Simone will have to get a letter from a *beast* that Ella's been eaten by *fish,* which does have a little bit of poetry to it, considering how many Ella's had to gut.

"Are you enjoying yourself, Ella?" Stanley asks.

"En-enjoying?" Ella gulps. They're trying to scare her to make her break the curse, she's sure of it, but now stubbornness and annoyance grapple with fear, and she won't agree. Not until she's in the goldfish's mouth.

Stanley shouts, "In the dungeon you said the only place *you'd* rather be is surrounded by hungry sharks. Unfortunately, we didn't have sharks."

"That was *sarcasm,*" Ella hollers. Her father was right. Her tongue keeps getting her into trouble.

"What's going on?" Neesa's words carry over the water. "Is this not what she wanted?"

"Why would I *want* this?" Ella glowers.

Neesa shoots a dangerous look at Stanley. "It did seem a little weird. Bring her back."

The little rowboat sways, and Ella shivers and squeezes her eyes shut. She'd imagined her life would flash before her, but all she's thinking about is that she would have preferred Simone to this, because at least at Simone's, she wasn't drowning.

Finally, the swaying stops, and Ella wonders if this is what death feels like.

She opens her eyes.

The boat is docked against the shore, the beast—Neesa—staring down with her green, unrelenting gaze.

Ella propels herself to solid ground, digging her bare toes into the earth and breathing heavy. She glares at the beast. Beneath the lion's head and the bear's body and the boar's tusks, it's hard to imagine there's a *girl,* but if Ella's good at anything, it's imagining.

"*What* was *that*?" Ella exclaims. Her hands are shaking from the cold and nerves, and she sticks them into her armpits.

"You're. Welcome," the beast says.

"I'm not going to thank you for almost drowning me," Ella snaps.

The beast growls, and Ella takes a step back.

"I was thanking *you,*" the beast says.

Ella stares at her. "I think you might need some help learning what a *thank-you* is."

"Stanley said you'd like it," the beast mutters.

"That's what *Ella* told *me,*" Stanley says defensively.

Ella's heart won't calm down. Her pulse batters her ears. She's still only half awake. All she knows is that she's so tired of other people and beasts and mice making decisions for her.

And she shoves the beast—Neesa—into the lake.

21

Ella

TO ELLA'S GREAT SURPRISE, NONE OF THIS results in her getting thrown back into the dungeon.

Instead Ella follows a dripping, fuming Neesa, a few pieces of lakeweed still clinging to her tusks, back into—

Ella rubs her eyes.

"Where are we?" Ella asks Stanley, forgetting to be mad at him about the boat.

This can't be the castle she was in yesterday. The wooden floor gleams, and sunlight spills upon light blue floral wallpaper, life-size golden statues of weeping willows that drape velvet leaves, tufted couches, and a little white harpsichord which—Ella jumps—starts to play a toccata by itself. The scent of honeysuckle wafts through the air.

Ella's not sure how she's supposed to break a curse if she can't keep track of what's happening.

"That's why we were trying to thank you," Stanley whispers, glancing at Neesa, who is scowling and rubbing herself dry with a tablecloth that Citrine has fetched. "The castle . . . is repairing itself. Like it did in your room."

"Is the curse broken?" Ella whispers. Is it that easy to end a curse after all? Just think about it and go to sleep?

"No," Stanley says. "But it's something."

"I can hear you."

Neesa prowls over to them, and Ella tries to keep her face calm and composed. She smells a little better, more like lavender, and a white bandage is wrapped around one forearm, but Neesa remains fearsome. She is nearly twice Ella's size, and her words slip out between a mouthful of sharp fangs.

"That wasn't very nice." Neesa scowls. "Pushing me into the lake."

Stanley makes a sound and rushes out, mumbling something about a snack.

"I wasn't trying to be nice," Ella retorts. "And you're not very nice, either."

"*I'm* not trying to be." Neesa bares her teeth. She looks like she's struggling to say whatever comes next. "But . . . what you did with the birds. You didn't need to do that."

Ella shrugs. She doesn't know how to explain that her father died, that her stepmother is cold and cruel, that she's spent so much time imagining adventures and she's not entirely sure what to do now that she seems to have found herself in one. And that she might not have claws, but she thinks she understands what Neesa is going through.

"Stanley told me you didn't steal the clock," Neesa continues. "That you risked yourself to help the old merchant."

Neesa stalks over to the window so Ella can only see the back of her shaggy head. "You can go back."

. . . Go?

Go. She's free. No curse-breaking involved. No risk of angering a fairy.

But where will Ella go? Back to the cellar, back to Simone and chores and her now-awkward, maybe spoiled friendship with Amir? The adventures she's yearned for aren't *back.* And now, here, a castle is blooming with magic. A beast is offering Ella the freedom of choice Simone never did.

Sure, breaking a curse might be dangerous, but don't all adventures include a little danger?

"Did you really do what everyone says? Kidnap maidens and travelers?"

Neesa snorts. "Absolutely not. Do you see any maidens or travelers?"

Well, aside from Ella? No.

"Where are you from?" Ella asks.

"What?" Neesa turns, surprised.

Most people probably don't ignore the chance to escape from a cursed castle.

"Stanley said you were . . . are . . . a girl. Where are you from?"

"He wasn't supposed to tell you that," Neesa grumbles.

"So?" Ella presses.

"Far away," Neesa finally says.

Ella's curiosity piques—she's eager to place Neesa on a map. "How far? As far as Apfel?"

"Farther."

"As far as the Sunset Isles?"

"It's a small village," Neesa relents, realizing that Ella is not going to stop. "It's not on most maps. It's called . . . Elsweyr."

Not on most maps. Ella's fingers itch, desperate to draw a map that *does* include it.

"Do you miss it?"

Neesa sniffs. "I miss the way things might have been," she says softly.

Something within Ella cracks wide open, like a seed that's finally burst to life. Both of their stories have gone wrong.

If Ella leaves, she's going to keep having the story she doesn't like. But if she stays . . . There are nine days left before Neesa is stuck as a beast. Nine days is a long time.

"You could probably use some help breaking the curse, couldn't you?" Ella asks.

"Miss—" Stanley, who has just returned with a plate of pumpkin cakes, stops short, eyes wide.

Neesa turns back from the window.

"What are you saying?"

"I'm saying that I think I'll stay a little longer," Ella says. "I'll help break your curse."

22

Belle

BELLE AND MARIE HURRY THROUGH THE market, dodging peddlers selling sprigs of rosemary and women smelling bouquets of flowers and men carrying trays of sourdough. They ignore the puppet show.

Truthfully, Belle was a bit worried about their plan. Once Marie discovered her and Amir in the alley, Amir had been quick to explain that he and Belle were going to find out what happened to Ella. Leave it to a prince to almost ruin Belle's escape attempt *twice*.

Belle had grappled with an overwhelming sense of dread; Simone would find out Belle was talking to a prince. Simone would be furious. Her commands would shrink Belle's freedom.

But instead Marie's face had brightened.

"Can I help?" she had asked. "Please *please please please* let me help."

"You can't tell Simone," Belle had warned.

"Are you kidding?" Marie clapped her hands. "This is the best secret I've ever had."

AMIR'S WAITING FOR THEM IN THE SAME ALLEY-way, perched on an overturned wooden crate, the cap pulled more firmly over his curls. He leaps up when he sees them, his cheeks popping with dimples.

Which is something Belle notices as a casual observer, and not because she's paying attention to his smile. And if she *was* . . . it's for research purposes only.

"You made it." Amir sounds almost relieved.

"So," Marie says. She looks completely unbothered to be speaking to a prince, even though Belle is sure Fiona would be choking with excitement. "How do we save Ella?"

"I have a few ideas," Belle says. That starts with the place where most secrets pass through.

They sneak into the post office when the postmaster is at lunch and sift through the ledgers, looking for any mention of Ella or the princess. Since Simone thinks Belle is just entertaining Marie, the manacle offers her a generous amount of freedom.

"Your sister's with an aunt on the Eastern Sea," Marie says, puzzled. "Isn't she? So why are we looking for her?"

"Because I haven't gotten a letter in three years," Amir says, looking embarrassed and hurt. "It was like with Ella. One day they were there. And the next they weren't."

But looking for clues isn't as successful as Belle expected, because she's used to doing this sort of thing with the help of magical objects, like the eyeglass that makes any letter with a mention of someone's name float in the air, or the whistle that would tell you what each letter writer was actually thinking.

Instead, all Belle can find is a surprising number of shipments of pumpkin cakes to the Dreamwood and an equally surprising number of love letters to an imprisoned troll.

Which reminds Marie that she's hungry and inspires her to fetch them tomato-mustard tarts, which they eat while working, careful not to spill on the ledgers.

"Five more minutes," Belle warns, glancing at the clock overhead.

"We're never going to figure out what happened to them." Amir slams his fists down onto the table.

Marie, by the window watching for the postmaster's return, glances at him, startled.

Belle frowns.

"We just got started," she says.

Amir glares.

"This is *impossible,*" he declares, but there's fear in his eyes, not anger. Belle recognizes it. She'd seen it in her father's face, when news of his wrecked ships kept coming, when the caravan's wheel splintered off as the debts kept piling up. Fear could so quickly devour hope.

"Stop being such a prince," Belle chides.

"What?"

Marie giggles.

"You're too used to things being easy," Belle pushes. "If it were easy to find missing princesses, no princesses would ever be missing. Any prince can sit around and complain. If you want to be a good one, maybe . . . spend more time *looking for evidence*."

Amir stares at her, but the edges of his lips crinkle into a smile.

"Captain Belle." Marie salutes.

After a moment, Amir salutes, too.

"Captain Belle," he says.

And Belle tells herself that the tingle in her chest is only glee that she's that much closer to getting her kiss, her locket, and her victory.

THE SECOND DAY, AMIR SHOWS UP TO THE ALLEY late, sweaty and disheveled.

"Fencing practice ran long," he explains, still panting. But, with a grin, he pulls out a crystal ball that he took from the Miravalian Palace.

"Before you ask, it's not my mother's," he says. "It's the cook's."

"Why would I ask that?" Belle wonders.

"Because . . . Because everyone always thinks my mother dabbles in dark magic."

"This isn't dark magic," Belle says with a scoff. "They practically give these away in other cities."

Amir flushes. "Well." He coughs and passes it to Belle. "I don't know what to do with it. But I thought you might?"

Belle grins.

She does indeed.

Belle runs her hands over the ball, whispers the words her father taught her to bring it to life. Gray smoke starts to spiral.

"Where's Ella?" she asks.

"Ella Aberdeen," Amir clarifies.

The gray smoke swirling inside remains gray and swirling.

Belle tries again. "Where's the princess?"

The smoke stays smoke.

Amir chews on the insides of his cheeks. It also refuses to reveal if the moon is made out of cheese, if Amir is a prince or a pelican, and if Marie is going to be a famous chocolatier.

"Maybe you got a bad one," Marie suggests. Belle doesn't tell Amir that she's not surprised; crystal balls are rarely better than party games.

But when she asks the crystal ball, at Marie's insistence, if Fiona is ever going to marry a prince, red smoke declaratively spells out, *No.*

Belle doesn't know what else to do but pat Amir, who's looking disappointed, on the head.

"At least that's one less thing you have to worry about," she says.

THE THIRD DAY, SIMONE ROLLS HER EYES AS Marie insists she and Belle go see the multicolored boats in Grimm Park, but she agrees after Marie warns the alternative is her loudly practicing the harpsichord.

Belle has to keep herself from yawning as she, Marie, and Amir make their way to the park. She'd stayed up the night before brainstorming.

Despite how Grimm Park sounds, it's bright and sunny, with a lake that people drift upon in rowboats and banks where picnickers are scattered.

"Over there." Belle points.

"That's *it*?" Amir asks, wrinkling his nose as they approach a full-length mirror at the edge of the park, propped up to eye level by an iron stand. The mirror's surface looks dirty, their reflections are twisted and oddly stretched, and its gold frame is tarnished. A plaque reads A MAGIC MIRROR, DONATION COURTESY OF LADY GRIMM.

"This doesn't actually work," Amir says. "Everyone knows that."

"It works," Belle assures him.

She knows because her father had appraised it for

Lady Grimm, a woman with a mysterious and murky reputation. That was one trip Henrik would not allow Belle to join him on. Henrik had returned, delighted, telling Belle about one of few magic mirrors that could show you anyone you asked to see, generously being donated to a public park.

"Your heart just has to be pure," she says, echoing Henrik. It was the only reason Belle didn't consider the mirror incredibly *creepy.* "Think of Ella. *Really* think of her. And it will show you where she is."

"Ella Aberdeen," Amir declares to the mirror, leaning closer, closer, his eyes widening, and then he huffs in annoyance. "It's not working," he declares, stepping aside.

Belle and Marie stare at their warped reflections. Marie tries, repeating Ella's name in the mirror, to the same result.

"Try someone whose location you know," Belle suggests. "Try your mother."

"Mother, um, Milan, um, Queen Milan?" Amir asks the mirror, and then gasps. This time when he steps aside, the mirror shows a crystal clear image of Queen Milan sitting near a pond, talking to the queen consort of Apfel, a dragon tattoo peeking out from her dress.

"Ella Aberdeen," Amir tries again.

Their warped reflections return.

"I'll go." Belle leans forward. "Henrik Villeneuve."

The mirror reveals a blurrier image of her father, sitting with a small group of what look like hunters in the Dreamwood. They're perched on rocks, eating. Belle exhales a worry she didn't know she had; he's okay. He just tumbled into another adventure on his way to her. But even as he chats, regaling them with a story, his smile never reaches his eyes, like some of his lightness had gone down with his ships.

Amir studies her briefly, before saying, "Anisa Perrault. The princess of Miravale."

A distorted Amir blinks back at him.

"What's happening?" he demands. "Why won't it work?"

There are only three things Belle can think: (1) there is powerful magic at play; (2) the girls are each too far away; or (3) like most magical objects with questionable owners, it's a bit fickle. There's a fourth option, but it's too dismal for her to think about. Her hypotheses are interrupted.

"We should go back," Marie reminds them. She's surprisingly practical, always the one to keep track of the time to make sure that Simone doesn't grow suspicious.

"I'm sorry that didn't work," Belle says as they return to the main avenue.

"It's closer to finding them than I've ever been." Amir's looking at Belle in a strange way. Marie, distracted by a family of quails, ignores them.

"What?" Belle asks.

"How'd you get that scar?" He points to the sickle-shaped mark on Belle's inner right arm.

Belle flushes. She didn't know he was paying that much attention to her. "A wyvern," she sighs. "It's a long story."

His strange look gets stranger. "You're not what I expected."

"Because I'm weird," she says.

He considers this, fiddling with his sleeves. "A *wyvern.* You just . . . You make the world seem bigger."

He's close enough that she can smell his soap, something with cedar.

Do it, she thinks, her heart hammering. *Do it and set me free.*

That's the only thing she's thinking. That's the only reason she wants him to lean forward even more.

But Amir pushes his newsboy hat farther down his curls and grins.

"Tomorrow," he promises. "Tomorrow we're going to find them."

THEY DON'T FIND THEM TOMORROW.

The fourth day is even less successful. As soon as Amir pops his head out of the alleyway to check if the coast is clear, there's a chorus of shrieking. Amir is tugged into a throng of people fawning over him.

Belle sighs. She doesn't have time to waste. The Revel is in less than a week. Six days until she needs to be free, locket around her neck, winning the Revel's contest.

She needs to help Amir. She needs to get her kiss.

That night Belle scribbles a message:

We'll find them.

—B

She surprises herself. Part of her wrote it to assure him and get closer to the kiss. Another part wrote it just to make him feel better.

Soon the dove returns.

I trust you.

—A

23

Ella

IT TURNS OUT THAT CURSES DON'T WANT TO be broken easily.

Nine days, Ella figured, was plenty of time to figure out how to break a curse. How tough can a riddle be, really?

After two days it becomes clear: very tough. The music room with its golden weeping willows becomes filled with torn-up scraps of paper. Theories are scribbled on the blue wallpaper and soon scratched out.

The first struggle is figuring out what the riddle even *means*. They decide upon: What does a thief steal if they've stolen nothing?

True love. (Too obvious.)

Moonlight.

Hunger.

Laughter.

True love. (Maybe being obvious means it's right?)

Ghosts.

Time.

Sleep.

Spiderwebs.

Garbage.

Air.

Kisses.

Nightmares.

Good dreams.

Dreams about cheese. (Stanley's contribution.)

Ella tests the theories by grabbing spiderwebs in her fists. She kisses the rose clock and brushes a kiss on Citrine's head and Stanley's and Neesa's cheeks. She breathes in the air deeply. She tries to nap, hoping to knock out sleep and some kind of dream all at once. But the riddle remains riddle-y.

Still, hope prevails. For the first time in what feels like forever, Ella wakes up in the softest bed she's ever known. The castle prepares delectable feasts, and Ella and Neesa eat in a room where sunlight splashes over a tiled floor and walls covered in painted flowers. At the long dining table, Ella insists they sit closer so they can brainstorm, and even though Neesa seems embarrassed, she soon learns that if she says the right joke at the right time, she can make milk spurt out of Ella's nose.

The days begin to tick down.

Nine.

Eight.

Seven.

Six days before the clock will stop, Neesa proposes a new theory: find the answer within the castle.

After all, the castle has transformed, unraveling seemingly endless splendors and rooms that now shimmer with light. The chandelier in the main hall shines bright over pillars painted with twining vines. The kitchen is a shining space staffed by no one, where a simple request will soon have a steaming apple cider or plate of lamb chops before you. There are giant tin soldiers that will carry you, if you ask politely—the statue-like shapes Ella had found so frightening her first day here, which had once taken her to the dungeons and back up to her room after Ella fell from the horse, Stanley explains.

The castle wasn't even this splendid when Neesa arrived, Ella learns, as if their shared imaginations built it into this. There are rooms made of pillows, rooms made of clouds, rooms made of candy. There are rooms that change color depending on your mood, an aviary filled with jeweled birds, though all are inanimate. A room that puts you at the center of a storm, a room surrounded by walls swishing with jellyfish. One room is painted dark blue with a giant telescope and a ceiling that opens. Ella wishes there were dwarfs to read the language of the stars to them.

Stars, they guess.

Feathers.

Thunderstorms.

Neesa and Ella take to exploring as they guess at the riddle, Ella occasionally wincing at the pain in her knee. They wander into telling their own stories.

How Ella ended up with Henrik, what life is like as a beast, although Neesa doesn't like talking about Elsweyr. She keeps details vague: a pond she liked swimming in, a market vendor she adored, how she liked to slip out at night to count the stars. Her life in the village was small, and her yearning to see Reverie matches Ella's.

"But what *were* you?" Ella presses.

Sometimes Neesa will say a jam seller or a horse trainer. Sometimes she'll storm away, caught in a dark mood. Something terrible must have happened with the fairy, and Ella resists asking more.

Pomegranates.

Fears.

They eat pomegranate seeds. In between, they listen to Stanley's lectures on his favorite types of cheese. Ella tries to teach Neesa how to make biscuits, but flour and claws aren't a good match. Neesa offers lots of ideas about how to deal with Miravale's goblin problem or the trade issues with Coralon. "I get bored," she mutters when Ella asks how she knows so much. Ella fears the curse, even when she doesn't want to, but her fear doesn't break it.

There are moments Ella forgets that Neesa's a beast.

Amir was one of her closest friends, and Marie wasn't bad, either, but Neesa understands her in a way no one else has.

Birdsong.

Any songs.

Music.

Silence.

Five days.

"WHY DIDN'T YOU GO BACK?" NEESA ASKS AS they poke around the gardens for clues. The grounds are also touched by magic. Green buds burst upward. The odd cream-white pomegranates have turned blush-pink, safe to eat and mixed with white cheddar, if Stanley's around.

Ducks float in the goldfish-filled lake, and the tin horses canter stiffly about. Ella avoids them, the memory of being thrown from one's back still too strong.

"Why didn't you go home?" Neesa repeats.

Ella feels uncomfortable. She likes Neesa thinking she is someone far more interesting than a scullery maid, and she's reluctant to tell the truth.

"My stepsisters used to call me Cinderella," Ella mumbles, explaining Simone and her chores, Fiona and her taunts, the cellar and the fish every morning.

"I thought you said you were friends with Amir," Neesa

presses. Ella warms a little; Neesa doesn't seem to care that Ella spent three years scrubbing floors and latrines. "He's the prince. Couldn't he help?"

Ella huffs. "Yeah. But . . . that's not how things work. And then I think I ruined it. . . . He . . . He tried to kiss me." The memory of that terrible thing makes her wince. She likes him, but not like that. It's horrible, how one small kiss can ruin so much. "He's probably glad I'm gone."

"I kissed a frog once," Neesa admits. "To try to break the curse."

They look at each other and burst out laughing. Neither Amir nor frogs, it turns out, are good for kissing.

"And . . . it's complicated," Ella adds. "Amir's sister . . . She's the reason my father lost his position." Ella scowls. She and Amir didn't talk about it. He loves his sister, and Ella hopes she will turn into a diseased rat. "I'll never forgive her for what happened."

"You forgave me," Neesa points out. "For locking you up. Right?"

"You're like me," Ella says. "You're trapped. You're *cursed.* The princess had everything, and all she did was hurt other people."

Neesa looks away. "Maybe she should have become a beast."

"I would have cursed her myself," Ella says sourly.

FOUR DAYS BEFORE THE CLOCK STOPS.

Ella stumbles into breakfast exhausted, and not just because Stanley had suggested she sleep outside with her pockets full of forks "stolen" from the castle, part of a curse-breaking theory Ella didn't fully understand. Her sleep has gotten worse as the date has gotten closer.

It was supposed to be easy to save Neesa. But now . . . Now every minute matters. Ella just doesn't know how to make sure they really count.

"You're not going to be any good at solving riddles if you're sleep-deprived and delirious," Neesa notes. But she seems like she's in good spirits.

Soon Ella discovers why.

Neesa leads them up a staircase that they haven't explored before, to an old medieval door. There's another small staircase next to it, although Neesa claims there's nothing up there.

"This is where we'll find the answer to the riddle." Neesa claps her paws in front of the door. "It'll be over by tonight."

But when Neesa shoves it open, they pause. The rest of the castle has been swept and restored by magic, but here the room is dim and smells like must. Everything looks half-destroyed.

"I don't think anything in here is going to help break a curse," Ella says, a little grouchy from sleepiness.

"Oh." Neesa swallows. "I thought it would have . . ."

"Here." Ella, regretting her sharp tongue, tugs the curtains open. At least that's a small thing she can do.

As if the castle has remembered itself, when the sunlight sweeps in, the cobwebs evaporate, the grime disappears from the shelves, and the dust spirals away. Dirt is swept from the floors, revealing tiles shaped like sunbursts. Where there were only shadows, there are now massive armchairs fit for a beast and an overstuffed couch beside a small fire.

"It's . . . perfect," Ella gasps.

The best part: shelves of books that go up and up and up, with a ladder propped against them. There are titles that Ella loves and titles in languages Ella didn't even know existed. On the walls not occupied by books or windows: maps of the underground, of the skies, of the seas, of cities, of ant colonies.

Ella feels—Ella feels alive.

Ella runs her fingers over the books' spines, possibility thrumming through her blood.

"My father would have loved it," she says. "*I* love it."

"I haven't been here in years," Neesa confesses, a little sadly.

"Years?" Ella asks. "How long have you been cursed?"

Ella worries that's a rude question to ask someone under an enchantment, but then she realizes that Neesa is thinking.

"Longer than I thought," she says, sounding surprised. "I stopped coming up here after the first few weeks."

During that time, no family visited her. There was only the occasional package of pumpkin cakes sent by her mother, Neesa revealed after Ella kept prodding her for details.

Reading a beast's face isn't as easy as reading a human's, what with all the extra fur and fangs, but Ella is learning. When Neesa's ears press back against her head, that means she's embarrassed.

And right now, they're very, very pressed back.

"I'm sorry," Neesa says. "For saying that you had to stay here forever. You've been . . . No one's been so nice to me in a long time."

"Forever only lasted a few days." The apology makes Ella blush.

Usually, Ella holds on to grudges, but she's having more fun than she's had for . . . well, probably for as long as Neesa's been a beast.

"But we *will* be stuck here forever if we don't focus on breaking the curse!" Ella declares.

They spend all day in the library, poring over books and maps, guessing.

Gravity.

Hope.

Anger.

Clouds.

Poetry.

They test out their theories. Ella runs outside to stare

long and hard at the clouds. She recites poetry from various books. She musters anger at Simone. She tosses the clock in the air to see if it will defy gravity and narrowly catches it before it crashes to the floor. Hope is already tightly wound around her heart.

The two of them scan books about the history of bees and how to make enchanted thimbles and the merpeople city at the bottom of the Vallian Sea, but a solution to the riddle remains elusive.

Stanley delivers cheese and crackers, then a bean-and-mutton stew, then pumpkin cakes as the hours bleed into night.

"Did you get to see any of these places?" Ella asks around a bite of mutton, tracing her finger over one of the maps. "Before?"

Neesa doesn't meet her eyes.

"No. I haven't been much of anywhere," she says, focusing on her stew. "I wasn't allowed to leave. The maps let me imagine I was somewhere else. Sometimes I think there's no point in breaking the curse if I'm just going to go from being trapped in a castle to trapped in a . . . village."

"I haven't gone anywhere, either," Ella says, wanting to cheer her up. "Maybe we can travel when the curse is broken. Together."

Neesa is so surprised, she knocks her stew over a book about a witch who created poisoned apples.

"Really?" She exclaims.

"I just . . ." Ella swallows, suddenly afraid Neesa will say she doesn't want to wander Reverie with her. She changes the subject. "We have to focus on the curse."

One minute they're trying to figure out if an ogre could be part of the riddle, and the next Ella is blinking herself awake, the room cozy with night, the fire burning low in the grate. Neesa is asleep beside her on the rug, snoring lightly.

Even though they're battling a curse and a countdown, Ella feels so *happy*. It's like a moment she hadn't known she was wishing for.

That's it.

A *wish*.

How does wishing fit into the riddle? She's not really sure, but she's not really sure how any of their guesses do. All she cares about is breaking the curse.

Still, Ella clenches her fists tight. She squeezes her eyes shut.

A wish a wish a wish a wish.

She says it in her head. And then aloud, little more than a whisper:

"I wish I wish I wish I wish."

Ella pries her eyes open, wishes flooding her.

But Neesa slumps beside her, still a beast.

24

Belle

THE MEADOWS," BELLE SUGGESTS.

The three are back in their usual alleyway, drinking fizzy lilac drinks that Amir bought. After several days of trying to solve the mystery of Ella and the princess, they have gotten sunburned, to Simone's dismay about Marie's increasing smattering of freckles, but Belle is starting to relish their afternoons. It makes her wish there wasn't an ulterior motive, or a magical manacle.

Marie scrunches her nose.

"The meadows? Is that . . . safe? What about goblins?"

"There could be Aster pixies in the meadows," Belle explains, inspired by the merchant selling fake pixies a few days before. "They love rumors. Maybe they heard something about Ella. Or Amir's sister."

"And there's no reason to worry about goblins," Amir chimes in, draining the last of his lilac drink. "They're really just misunderstood."

That's not entirely true, Belle knows. It depends on the goblin. Some goblins, yes, are very kind and love tea parties where they gossip and tell you Reverie's affairs. Goblins have a staggering amount of knowledge, far more wisdom and rumors than their pixie cousins. Other goblins are bloodthirsty and worth avoiding, and while besting one in combat entitles you to learn one of its secrets, only the very foolish would resort to that. Belle and Henrik had dined with the nicer sort of goblin just outside of the Ridgewood Swamp while narrowly escaping the less-nice sort in the Ambrosian Sands.

"Goblins won't come so close to city gates," Belle blurts out. She's not entirely sure, although she's probably right.

She's starting to get desperate, and Aster pixies are her last chance. There are only three days left before the Revel. If Amir doesn't kiss her . . . She won't let herself think about that, although the manacle never lets her forget as she scrubs latrines in the evenings and mashes blueberries into jam and has to watch Fiona practice curtsying, to perfect it for the next time Amir comes for dinner.

The three of them edge out of the alleyway, Amir keeping his head down. It's slow working their way through the marketplace. They're extra careful to avoid attention after the other day, and it's extra crowded for the coming Revel.

"I wish it wasn't happening," Amir groans. "All it's

going to be is people making a fuss over me because they hope I'll give them something."

"You could always just declare a champion now," Belle says. "Get it over with."

"The most I could give them would be . . . my hat." He pats his newsboy cap. "I have to announce the winner, but my parents are the ones who actually *award* anything."

Belle sighs. It was worth a try.

"You're *sure* we don't have to be worried about goblins?" Marie confirms.

"It's fine," Belle assures her. Probably.

"When I'm king," Amir declares, "I'm going to let every goblin come to Miravale for a festival so people see they're not so bad."

Belle decides that she might need to give him a proper warning before he gets the crown.

Amir drops a few coins into a merchant's cup in exchange for a small box of dates. He extends them to Marie and Ella. "Try these. They're from my mother's city. And these." He drops more coins into a baker's cup for a basket of pumpkin cakes. "These were my sister's favorite."

Soon Belle's mouth is singing with sugar, and everything seems infinitely possible.

A meadow is romantic. Even if they don't find Amir's sister and Ella, maybe the setting would be right. . . . She could bat her eyes, or dazzle him with her knowledge of gnome cuisine, or do whatever Fiona wouldn't, and then tear off the manacle herself.

But beneath the sweetness, a sourness blooms; she hates that she'll be tricking Amir, just another girl using him for his princeliness.

As Amir steers them away from the market, the homes shrink and the streets quiet. Here the pink stone houses are one story with thatched roofs. Chickens squawk, and a few goats chew on grass. A woman kneels in the dirt, plucking beets. Marie stops to pet every cat napping in the late-afternoon sun.

Belle saves her pumpkin cake for last and nibbles at the soft dough, the sweet pumpkin cream inside.

"If you're part of Villeneuve Trading, why are you working as Simone Steinem's servant?" Amir trots up beside her.

Belle glances at Marie, who is thoroughly engrossed in watching a goat eat a tin can.

"It's a long story," she says, hoping he won't say more. He must read something on her face because he asks instead, "Have you ever been to the Hall of Clouds? With your father? I've always wanted to go."

A prince he may be, Belle's learning, but he's hardly seen any of the world. The king and queen are strict, keeping him nearly constantly within castle walls, especially after the princess left, and he seems famished for stories.

"Why don't you leave more?" Belle wonders.

"It's hard, isn't it?" he asks. "To do what you want *and* what your family wants?"

Belle busies herself with the last of her pumpkin cake.

It's a funny feeling to find someone who shares your thoughts.

They approach the pink gates between Miravale and the meadows, which were designed by a previous king to keep magical creatures from entering Miravale without permission.

"Belle . . . I'm . . . I'm worried that something bad happened to my sister." Amir's voice drops. "Mother won't talk about it, and Father certainly won't, but . . . I haven't had a letter from her. And the fog in the mirror . . . What if . . . ?"

He hovers before the gates. He's afraid to go out there and get answers, Belle realizes, in case those answers aren't what he wants.

"I'm sure they're fine." After all, Ella has a fairy godfather, and as far as Belle's aware, the reign of terror of the beast of the woods is only gossip. "And the Aster pixies will help."

They pass through a small gate and enter the meadows. Wildflowers twist in the breeze, and squirrels race up tree trunks. Just beyond a paved stone path, the tall pines mark the start of the Dreamwood. Belle's heart stretches for it.

They're the only ones in the meadows, an odd trio on an even odder quest.

"Maybe everyone's scared of the goblins," Amir observes, shedding his cap and running a hand through his hair. "Now. How do we find these pixies?"

"Look for pixie rings," Belle instructs, describing the circle of white funnel-shaped mushrooms that mark a colony.

Marie clambers up a tree, trying to see if she can spot some in the distance, and Amir hunts along the ground, sifting aside clovers and rocks. Belle joins him.

"We shouldn't have to hunt for the pixies," Amir mutters. "When I'm king, magical creatures will be allowed in Miravale again. Maybe the only reason the beast of the woods is so angry is because it has to be 'of the woods.'"

"A lot of people are afraid of magic," Belle says. Being afraid of magic—real magic, not what costs a few coins at a market—is practical. It's finicky, unpredictable, dangerous. And it's wonderful.

"You aren't," Amir says. "What would you do?"

Belle shrugs. "I'm not the queen."

Marie wanders over to them, frowning. A few leaves are ensnared in her red curls, and the sleeve of her orange dress has torn. "I couldn't see any," she says, but Amir's gaze is intent on Belle.

"Say I marry you and make you queen," he says. "Then what would you do?"

"What's in it for me, being queen?" Belle asks. This conversation feels like someone lit a match inside her chest.

Only because it's my way out, she reminds herself. *Kiss me now. Let me get to the Revel.*

"I would pay you to marry him," Marie chimes in. "Just to make Fiona lose her mind."

"You would have to be *bribed* to marry me?" Amir's eyes sparkle.

"I'm very practical." Belle grins. "I'm not letting the royal coffers go to waste."

"And we ain't, neither," a rusty voice grates.

Chills drip down Belle's neck.

Hulking creatures surround them, dusty blue skin pulled taut over bulging muscles and sneering skulls. They're protected by little more than loincloths, but they don't need armor; their hides are as tough as a soldier's best shield.

Spittlc drips from curved fangs.

"What kind of ransom do you think we'd get for you three?" the biggest, bulkiest one asks, pointing a knife at Amir's throat. "Or is a princeling better on a spit?"

Belle's heart thuds between her feet.

Goblins. And not the nice kind.

25

Ella

THE MOOD IN THE LIBRARY SHIFTS AS DRAmatically as a storm sweeping in.

Ella and Neesa, with Stanley chiming in and bringing almond tarts, dive into stories of curses and famous curse-breakers, men and women who hawked their services around Reverie for dizzyingly high sums. As they search, it becomes painfully clear that some curses are never broken. Those under them are trapped enchanted. Forever.

Neesa slams a book shut, storming out of the room. Ella puts her head down on the table and tries wishing again, but all that happens is Stanley sneezes.

Three days remain.

26

Belle

THE GOBLINS SURROUND BELLE, MARIE, AND Amir, cackling and sniffing the air. There are at least five, although Belle doesn't dare look toward the Dreamwood in case she sees more of their yellow eyes gleaming through the trees.

"Let's start with this one. Looks the plumpest." One slobbers, jabbing a long, dirty fingernail into Marie's arm. Belle expects her to burst into tears, but she spits directly into the goblin's face.

"Appetizer," it growls, but Marie doesn't flinch.

Amir has frozen. He barely breathes as the rusted dagger threatens to dig into his neck.

Belle's mind churns.

Really, the only way to escape a goblin attack is to run very fast or—

That's it.

Belle bolts.

With Amir and Marie still surrounded, Belle surges across the grass, trampling wildflowers, and back through the gate into Miravale.

She hears their howls of dismay, the goblin's harsh laughter.

"Cowards taste too bitter, anyway," a goblin snickers.

Just you wait, Belle thinks as the city gate clangs shut behind her.

She lunges toward the closest yard, vaulting over the fence and stuffing a very surprised rooster under one arm. Without stopping to take a breath, Belle spins on her heel, pushes away a few pieces of brown hair that have fallen in front of her face, and races back to the meadow.

Goblins don't fear much, but they are afraid of one thing.

Roosters.

She expects to see Amir and Marie at the goblins' mercy, but the creatures are in a state of mayhem, shrieks and yells tearing through the air. Marie is chasing one of them through the meadows, thwacking at it with a tree branch, and Amir has somehow managed to wrestle the knife away from the goblin, jabbing it at any creature that gets too close to him.

"You didn't leave us," Amir gasps to Belle, and in the

moment of distraction, the goblin wins the knife back from him. But it doesn't look gleeful. It just looks angry, raising the blade above Amir.

Uttering a silent apology to the rooster, Belle throws the bird in their midst.

The goblins freeze. The one near Amir drops its hand, the dagger slicing Amir's arm. The goblin fleeing from Marie lowers into a crouch.

The rooster crows, fluffing its wings and pecking at the ground.

The goblins scatter, three of them sprinting back to the woods.

Belle grins. In goblin lore, roosters possess dreadful powers, capable of turning them into stone. Belle isn't sure if this is true, but she's glad the goblins believe it is.

"You little witch," the biggest one growls at Belle while pacing backward. The rooster hops toward it, squawking, and the goblin leaps away. "You've made an enemy tonight."

"I hope not," Belle says, and she holds up her empty hands. A goblin sign of deference. She wouldn't willingly hurt anything, not even a goblin. They're just doing what goblins do. "I was only trying to protect us. But . . . *wait.*"

Belle's remembered a fact she never thought she'd put into use.

"You owe us a secret. It's only fair."

She can't wait to tell Henrik that she bested one of

the nastier types of goblins to win a piece of knowledge. Maybe he'll finally understand that she can hold her own. Belle feels Amir's gaze, and if she dared to peek, she wonders what she'd find there.

The goblin looks like it's about to curse her, but then it bows its head just slightly. "Clever girl," it says. "What do you want to know?"

"What happened to Ella?" Belle asks. "And the prince's sister?"

"One question!" the goblin shrieks, eyeing the rooster warily.

"My sister." Amir strides forward, eyes fiery. "What happened to my sister?"

"There is no beast of the woods!" The goblin cackles and dashes into the Dreamwood.

This goblin, it appears, prefers nonsense to secrets.

"What?" Amir mutters.

"Yeah!" Marie screams, shaking her fist in the air. "Take that!"

Belle stares after the goblins, tapping the spot where her locket used to hang.

"We should get out of here. Hurry, hurry!" Amir says, picking up the rooster and handing it to Belle, and they race back through the city gates.

They only pause so Amir can secure the gate and Belle can deposit the rooster back in its yard, its angry squawking causing dogs up and down the street to start barking. Marie glances back, her lips drawn tight.

Amir clutches his bleeding arm to his chest. The walls and meadows beyond are silent, but Belle is snapping with adrenaline, and the sudden peacefulness of the city feels like a trap.

"It's not so bad," he promises Belle, who's staring at his arm. "And the court healer will take care of it."

But that's not the only thing Belle is concerned about. Her chance for freedom is over. You can't lead a prince into a goblin nest, get him sliced by a dagger, and expect him to thank you with a kiss.

"I'll alert the guards that the goblins are there!" Amir says. "Now go, go!"

There is so much Belle wants to say, apologies to share, but there's no time. They need to get back, to put more walls between them and the goblins. Belle takes Marie's hand, and they dash through the empty streets, across cobblestoned roads and the nighttime ruins of the market. They run even when Belle's lungs and feet burn and she's sure Marie's do, too, in her ridiculous little slippers.

Finally, they approach the Steinems' town house. A lamp spills warm light over the door and its rosemary bundle, and Belle feels heavy with consequences. She was so sure the meadows would be safe, and now she's injured a prince.

"I'm sorry. That was all my fault," Belle whispers, clutching Marie's forearm before they enter. Marie glances down at Belle's grip, the manacle of obedience glinting in the lamplight. "But please don't tell Simone."

“You better hurry,” Marie says tonelessly, and Belle has no idea what she’s thinking. If she’ll reveal Belle’s friendship with Amir. If somehow word will get back to the royal family that Amir has been sneaking out. “You don’t want Mama to catch you out here.”

27

Ella

WHEREVER ELLA GOES, SHE HEARS TICKing clocks.

Tick . . . Tick . . . Tick . . .

There's one more day before the clock stops.

Ella's not sure where the time went. Into riddle guesses that never amounted to anything more, into stories of the trips they would take to the Vallian Sea.

She wakes early, when the sun is still shy and the castle's hallways are quiet. She patters down them.

One day. That's not great. But that's not terrible.

You can break curses in a day.

Hot peppermint tea waits in the library for her, just as a clean pink dress had been waiting in her closet.

"Thank you," she whispers to the castle.

If she's going to find answers, it will be in this room. She is her father's daughter, after all.

Except her father had decades of practice. Ella is simply baffled by the sheer number of books, and the library starts to seem less like an oasis and more like a maze. How they can find an answer to a riddle here is—

But maybe it's not about finding answers.

Maybe it's about finding the creature who has them.

A fairy is behind Neesa's curse, which means a fairy should know how to end it. It seems so obvious.

Ella tears down every book she can find on fairies, but no matter how much she reads, there's hardly anything useful. Apparently, fairies don't like to be written about. All Ella can find is that they love a good party. It's like they're intentionally mocking her.

Ella groans. Even if she *is* the false thief, the curse seems unimpressed. Maybe she ought to throw the curse a party for being so frustrating.

"I found her, Miss Neesa!"

Tiny mouse feet trot over the library's marble floors. Ella has missed the entire start of the day. The sky is flush with midmorning gold, and Ella's stomach gurgles.

Stanley straightens his vest. "You weren't at breakfast," he informs Ella.

Neesa follows, hovering in the doorway.

"I thought you'd left," Neesa says. "I wouldn't blame you."

Because then Ella might escape whatever happens when the clock stops.

Ella gestures at the pile of books in front of her. "I got distracted," she apologizes. "I was looking for fairies."

A cloud falls over Neesa's face.

Ella's gotten more familiar with Neesa's moods, but it always surprises her when they strike. When she's annoyed that Ella beats her at cards. When the sparrows won't nibble on the birdseed she's made. Ella isn't sure if this is a consequence of being a beast for so long or a glimpse of the girl she used to be.

"And did it help?" Neesa snaps. "Or has it been like every other day we've wasted in here?"

"It's only wasted if you want to stay a beast forever," Ella counters.

"Surely there must be something," Stanley says.

"You think I haven't tried?" Neesa argues. "When this happened, you think I didn't read every book on fairies that I could?"

Ella feels cold. She thought she was so smart to look for fairies, but Neesa had beaten her to it. A world's worth of books, but nothing for Neesa.

"Fresh eyes," Stanley suggests.

"You could get all the eyes in the world, but they can't read what doesn't exist," Neesa barks.

Ella's mind ticks. Fairies don't want their secrets written down. Neesa is right; the answer can't be found by *reading*.

"That's it," Ella gasps. "We need to catch a fairy."

28

Belle

THE PROBLEM WITH THE RADISHES IS THAT they're radishes.

It would be much better if they were turnips. In the Dreamwood, the Fairy of Flora and her ward taught Belle how to mix them with fly amanita to make a serum that could mute magic, like the bracelet. But she doesn't have turnips, or mushrooms, for that matter.

Belle kneels in the garden, brushing dirt off the scrawny radishes and tossing them into a metal pail, and trying not to panic. The Revel and the competition are tomorrow, and all she can do is weed. The manacle pinches her, forcing her to weed a little faster.

She hasn't heard from Amir—the papers suggest that the goblin attack sparked tighter security at the palace—

and Marie has barely spoken to Belle since. Guilt gnaws at her; she's used to danger, but she didn't have any right to drag them into it. But after spending so much time with Amir and Marie, being alone feels lonelier than ever. And for what? Goblin deception and nonsense?

"Did you not hear the bell?" Simone's shadow stretches long over the garden and its scraggly harvest. "I rang. You don't think coffee pours itself, do you, girl?"

"Sorry, Simone." Belle drops into a low curtsy but does not head to the kitchen. Simone's question isn't officially a command. "There was something I wanted to ask you."

"*I* ask. You do." But Simone looks intrigued, and eventually, she waves her hand and snaps, "Ask, then. Since I'm already out here."

"I want to go to the Revel of Spectacles." Belle winces around the words.

Asking Simone is the last thing she wants to do, but she's running out of options. And she has to get to the Revel.

Simone bursts out laughing. "You? Go to the Revel of Spectacles? *You?* A servant girl?"

Belle bristles. She's not a servant, and it shouldn't matter if she were.

"Everyone's invited," she points out through gritted teeth. "It wouldn't be odd if I came."

Simone's gaze rakes over Belle's dirt-covered apron and dress. "You can go to the Revel with us if you help me finish my outfit. Appearances matter, you know."

"Anything," Belle promises. And she'll do it. She really will.

"Nothing stops you, does it?" Simone asks. "I admire that. Let's see. . . . Pick a blooming rose from this garden for me to wear to the Revel. And it must be from *this* garden." Simone's gaze slides to the bracelet. "I'll know."

Belle stares at her. Impossible. No roses bloom in this garden, and none certainly will by tomorrow.

"Anything else," Belle chokes out.

Simone shrugs. "I thought you were supposed to be so clever."

Belle stares at her and feels absolutely, horribly trapped.

"Surely," Simone says, "surely, you can manage something as simple as picking a rose?"

29

Ella

TO CATCH A FAIRY, YOU NEED THREE THINGS.

You need a wish, of course. But a wish alone won't necessarily gain a fairy's attention. As Ella has noticed, given all the unanswered wishes she's had recently.

You also need a pot of honey to attract them; fairies love sweet things.

And you need the dreams of a lacewing butterfly, to bind them in place for several minutes; fairies crave impossible things.

Honey is easy enough to find. The larders of the enchanted castle are well stocked, and Ella and Neesa bring out not just a pot of honey, but entire barrels, hoping to get on the fairy's good side.

The wish, of course, is simple, and Ella's already practiced her wishing: they want to break the curse.

They don't know the specific fairy that cursed Neesa, though any fairy will do, they reason. They all have magic.

But Ella and Neesa spend the entire afternoon roaming through the gardens, looking for a butterfly, and when they capture one they think might be a lacewing, they spend several hours wondering how to make a butterfly fall asleep, and then how you go about making sure the dreams don't just drift away.

Eventually, Ella and Neesa accept defeat and let the maybe-lacewing go. If it had dreamed, the dreams had vanished wherever they vanish to, without the two of them noticing.

There are easier ways, of course. Not all fairies are this tricky. In the Dreamwood, the Fairy of Flora answers wishes-with-a-capital-*W* Wishes, crafting potions and serums to grant your desire. But her wishes require time, if she even pays attention to your wish in the first place.

Neesa flops onto the sofa in the library, and Ella stretches herself out in front of the fire. It crackles with heat, warming her arms.

"Maybe we can just try to use our own dreams," Ella suggests. "Maybe the fairy won't notice."

"Maybe. But. There's also . . ." Neesa clears her throat, like she's coughing up a hair ball. Her claws draw circles on the sofa. "A, um, a town not far from here. There's an alchemist. He might have the dreams. The curse won't let me leave the grounds, but . . ."

Even if Neesa and Stanley could leave, it's not as if there were many places they could go. A talking toy mouse and a beast can't wander into a town. That's the start of a bad joke that ends with pitchfork-armed villagers.

The problem with catching a fairy is much the same as the problem with trying to break a curse: it can go awry. Fairy-catching isn't exactly legal, with all the ways it could backfire. Ella once heard a story of someone who tried to catch a fairy to force her to make him the wealthiest man in Reverie, and he ended up turning an entire village into beetles.

If someone suspected what they were doing, there could be guards. Magistrates. They could contact Simone, and Ella doesn't want to think about what kind of measures Simone would take to make sure Ella doesn't get out of the cellar again.

The risks of going are high. But the risks of staying safe are much higher.

Ella rubs her glass leg. Her father sacrificed, and Henrik explored, just so she could have it, and she wants to be worthy. When she first got her leg, she was so scared of shattering it, she hardly left the house. Now there are plenty of reasons to be afraid of leaving the castle. But what would happen if Ella didn't fear being shattered?

"I'LL BE BACK BY NIGHTFALL," ELLA PROMISES. She, Neesa, and Stanley stand at the edge of the castle grounds near the wall of roses. The sun is sinking in the sky and turns the white roses gold.

Staring at the path ahead, Ella winces. Navigating the Dreamwood alone, convincing an alchemist to sell her a rare ingredient, avoiding the curious looks of the city guard . . . Part of her wishes she could take back her offer to go into the village. Sit by the fire instead, nibbling on almond muffins. But not breaking the curse is much more frightening than venturing by herself.

"There's nothing to worry about out there," Neesa promises. Ella adjusts a cloak Neesa had lent her. It's silky and light, as marvelous as everything in Neesa's castle now. "The Dreamwood is completely safe."

"Before dark," Stanley corrects. "And if you stay on the path."

"And you'll find your way back," Neesa reminds her. "Anyone who knows where the castle is can return."

"It's not that." Not *just* that. Without thinking, Ella bends down to rub the knee above her glass leg, anticipating the ache of such a long walk.

"What's wrong?" Neesa asks.

"Nothing." Ella doesn't like people knowing that she hurts. She sharpened her tongue so no one would know when her heart ached, and she made herself seem strong so no one would know when her leg made her feel weak.

She's done a good job so far of not letting Neesa see how much her leg throbs after their days exploring the castle.

Neesa's eyes are bright and thoughtful. She tears a white rose from the wall, extending it to Ella.

"As long as you wear it, it'll take away your pain," Neesa says. "When I first . . . When this first . . ." She motions at her body. "It hurt a lot. I wore a rose until I got used to it."

When Ella tucks the rose into her dress and shifts her weight onto her glass leg, she feels no pain.

"They're enchanted," Neesa explains. "By the Fairy of Flora. When I was first brought here."

Ella shrugs like it doesn't matter that much, but her eyes sting. Sometimes small kindnesses can seem impossibly big. And how wrong everyone in Miravale was; they feared a bloodthirsty beast, and here Neesa was, receiving gifts from fairies who pitied her. There can be so many different versions of the same story.

"Hurry," Neesa says. "Before the alchemist's shop closes."

Ella wanders past the space where magic sucks away all sound, and the woods are as beautiful as she remembers. Birds twitter in the trees. Shards of sunlight illuminate little mushroom men toddling through the overgrowth, ruby-red lizards as long as Ella's thumb, secrets carved into tree trunks. For once, her imagination can't outpace her.

After a while, the path forks, and Ella veers to the right, stepping out of the Dreamwood. Kindlecrest is not all that far from Neesa's castle, part of the Miravalian kingdom, but it seems like a different world.

Ella knows Kindlecrest from her father's maps, and she keeps expecting to hear him explain its agricultural industry, its famous beef pastries.

The buildings are painted white with limestone and have thatched roofs. The dirt paths are slightly red, and mules pull carts laden with canvas sacks as people mill about, preparing for the end of the day. A few chickens cluck around an outdoor café. Ella swallows her nerves.

She's been a terrible, rotten curse-breaker so far. What if she can't do something as simple as get a butterfly's dreams?

Even here, Revel preparations are underway. People hammer purple banners and ribbons above windows. Outside a pub men are crouched in the dirt, taking bets on what the Revel's competition will be. Ella can smell a distant bonfire and hears cheers; someone must be preparing to head to the Revel to try their hand at the competition.

She had almost forgotten it was tomorrow. She's relieved she doesn't have to be part of all the pomp and silliness.

Aided by the townspeople, who stare at her as if she's grown a third eye, Ella finds the alchemist's shop. It's at the edge of Kindlecrest, where ducks quack and plum trees drip heavy with fruit.

At first, Ella worries that the shop is closed. But the door opens when she presses upon it, with an exhale of herbs. The shop is small but cluttered, windows largely blocked by overstuffed cupboards.

"It does no good, getting involved with fairies," a voice warns, followed by a series of dry coughs. A small, bent figure shuffles out of a space between the cupboards, blinking from behind thick spectacles.

A fist tightens around Ella's heart.

"What? No fairy!" Ella exclaims. "I don't know any fairy!"

"You come from the woods." The alchemist ignores her. "I can see it on your boots, and I can smell it on you."

Ella sniffs herself. She supposes she does smell a little . . . wood-y.

"I was helping my mother in the yard," Ella says, a lie they had rehearsed. "That's all."

"You have nothing to fear from me." The alchemist taps one of the shelves. "You are not the first to come here looking for a cure to a curse. And you are not the first to leave here disappointed."

"Then don't let me leave here disappointed," Ella says, prickling slightly. He doesn't have any right to treat her like a clueless girl. "Because I'm not interested in curses. I need the dreams from a lacewing butterfly."

The alchemist smiles at Ella and shakes his head slightly.

"The lacewing butterfly . . . interesting. A bold approach."

"It's for my father," Ella adds hastily. "For his snoring."

The alchemist ignores her, riffling among the small jars,

finally selecting one that has a thin layer of what looks like clouds but moves like oil.

"No charge," he says, handing the jar to Ella. "I wouldn't mind hearing about a bit of spectacular magic. But be careful, my dear. It's my last one, and a rare thing at that."

Ella hurriedly thanks the alchemist, rushing out before he changes his mind and stuffing the vial of butterfly dreams into her cloak. There's no time to waste. Now that she has it, now that it's real, the tick-tick-ticking of the clock inside her head gets worse.

Outside, dusk has fallen. The sky is streaked with purple and black, and the earliest stars are beginning to glimmer. Ella rubs her hands over goose bumps. At least her leg doesn't hurt as she sets out at a fast trot back.

Within the next few hours, Neesa will be a girl again. And she'll invite Ella back home or to wander Reverie with her. Neesa hasn't *said* that she can come, but surely she'll understand that Ella can't go back to Simone. It all seems so close and so real that she can almost smell Elsweyr, which Ella imagines smells like wisteria and vanilla.

Ella passes a tavern, where three young men are shouting at a round table about heading to the Revel tomorrow, mugs sloshing with golden ale.

"It's a little late for a fair maiden to be wandering alone, isn't it?" a large man with long, glossy hair cries, and Ella realizes with a lurch that he's talking to her. "Come, wish us good luck before the Rev— Where are you going? The Dreamwood isn't safe at this hour."

Ella ignores him. To make herself feel braver, she imagines she is a fairy queen, one so powerful that she can turn men into frogs with a flick of her fingertips.

"The Dreamwood is a dangerous place for a young girl," the man calls again.

"You hear some quite nasty stories," sneers a tall, twitchy man.

"Miss? Miss?" calls a teapot of a man, short and stout, with greasy black hair plastered over his head and a red bandanna around his neck. "Hey, Maximus, Lucan, we have to stop— You can't enter the Dreamwood, miss! It's not safe after dark!"

Footsteps behind her. Apparently, they can't tell just how wrathful a fairy queen can be.

Ella hurries, passing underneath the boughs of pines and firs. Safe during the day, Stanley had said. Well, there was still a sliver of day. And staying on the path is something she can do.

"Haven't you heard about the beast that lives in those woods?" the large man calls.

"Don't frighten her, Maximus," another man huffs.

"I've heard the beast prefers pumpkin cakes to *fair maidens*," Ella spits. As if a man like him could frighten her.

But she feels faintly ill. She can't let the man and his friends follow her back to the castle. If they found it . . .

"Why does she keep running?" one of the men huffs. "Why are we even bothering?"

"We can't let her get hurt!" another argues, and Ella does not understand how any of this is their business.

"You're lucky enough to have met the future winner of the Revel of Spectacles!" Maximus declares. "We will safely escort you out of this treacherous place!"

Ella has a head start, but the men are fast.

She has no choice.

She can't let Maximus and his friends find the castle. She can't let them find Neesa.

She veers off the path, slipping among ferns and vines and ducking under tree branches.

At first nothing changes. It's the same peaceful, quiet Dreamwood. But even as she tells herself this, a rustling begins and gets louder. It's a big rustling.

The kind that belongs to something much larger than a fox or a skunk.

And then an unmistakable howl.

30

Belle

THE NIGHT BEFORE THE REVEL, AFTER THE radishes are picked (by Belle), the parlor curtains cleaned (by Belle), dinner served (by Belle) and eaten (not by Belle), and the dishes cleared away (again by Belle), Belle rushes to the garden. The entire day, her mind has been filled with roses.

Belle throws herself before the bushes and pulls aside the stems as delicately as she can, though a few thorns still manage to prick her. There isn't the hint of a bud, but Belle has to figure it out. She just has to. She won't be foiled by flowers.

"Are you . . . gardening?"

Belle jumps. Amir leans against the garden wall, nudging a rock with his boot. She's surprised by the burst of relief and joy at seeing him.

"There she is," he says. "The Great Goblin Slayer."

"No," she says quickly. "I threw a rooster."

"Even better," Amir says. He nods to the gate. "Come with me."

"Even after last time?" Belle asks.

She'd been worried that he hated her for leading them into a nest of goblins, the way Marie seems to.

"Consider this the favor you owe for almost killing me." Amir grins. "C'mon. We've only got a bit before the guards realize my slumbering body is a pile of pillows." He pauses. "Next thing you know, my parents will be using their sleeping potion on me."

"They got it to work?" Belle asks, thinking how much simpler this would all have been if Plan Sleeping Potion had worked out.

"Not at all," Amir says. "They made a trade with some witch who offered to help. If you ask me, it wasn't really on the up-and-up."

"Just promise this adventure of yours doesn't require us testing it out," she teases. Amir grins.

This is it. Her way out. The Steinems are asleep. The Revel is tomorrow; all she needs is a kiss tonight. With the manacle off, she can slip back into the house, steal the locket, and be ready for the competition before anyone's the wiser.

"Coming?" Amir asks.

"What kind of favors have to be done in the dark?" Belle asks.

"The very secret kind," Amir promises.

They walk along the main avenue, and Amir peppers her with questions about the Glacial Halls, like nothing has changed, like he doesn't hate her after the goblins. Belle asks him about the Revel and the competition, but Amir knows nothing; it's his father's concern.

No one pays them any attention. The people who are out at this hour are either returning from the tavern or hatching dangerous plots. Still, while Amir tries to saunter down the middle of the street, Belle steers him into the shadows, noticing a pack of rat-faced men glancing at them and muttering.

"Are you going to tell me what we're doing out here?" Belle whispers.

"Again, top secret."

"But—is that . . . a sewer? What's going on?"

Because—yes. Amir has led them down a side alley and is twisting off a sewer grate.

"It's the safest place. Was," Amir says, with all the confidence of a prince who doesn't have a lot of experience actually needing to worry about safe places. "Are you coming?"

Belle swallows. There's a stench rising from the sewer, but she'll do what it takes to get her kiss.

And, if she's being honest, she's curious.

She steps through the grate, Amir close behind.

To Belle's relief, it doesn't smell as bad as she expected. It's mostly dry, only a thin ribbon of dirty water sloshing down the middle. Belle's skin tingles and she pauses. There's magic around.

"Amir . . . ," she begins, but he's charging ahead, stopping near a bend to shift aside what looks like rubbish and furniture parts and filthy rags.

He pulls out a pair of glittering shoes.

Belle peers closer.

No. Not glittering. They're entirely—

"Glass slippers," Belle whispers in awe.

Not even Henrik has seen a pair before. They're very rare, enchanted to make the wearer unrecognizable and confuse anyone who sees them, originally used by spies and thieves. There are stories of forbidden loves, infiltrated balls, fallen empires . . . Few objects have such a romantic and tragic history.

"They were my sister's. A gift from the Duchess of Salt," he explains, flushing a little. "I hid them down here when she disappeared. My father destroyed a lot of magical objects after he sent Ani to our aunt. These were the only things I could grab. I didn't want them to get lost."

"Why are we getting them now?" Belle asks, restraining her desire to shove them on and see if they work.

"I was going to give them to Ella—she has this glass leg, and I thought it might be nice . . . but now . . ." His bushy eyebrows dance as he talks. "My sister never liked them. So . . . they're yours."

With a kiss and glass slippers, she'll have no problem thieving back her locket. It's like fortune is finally smiling on her.

"Why?" Belle gapes. As Amir holds them out to her,

their fingers brush. He holds his hands there longer than he needs to.

Even in the sewer's dark, Belle sees a flush rise on Amir's cheeks and hopes that he can't see it on hers.

"Because I don't think you're just here to help Simone. You're up to something mysterious," he says. "And these seem like they could be helpful. Anyway. Every goblin slayer deserves an award."

These are exactly what she needs; she can sneak into Simone's house, forgettable, and steal back the locket. It just might work.

"Rooster thrower," Belle corrects softly.

"Defender of Miravale," Amir corrects again. "Every prince needs one."

But before Belle can respond, voices yell and feet pound right outside the storm drain.

"I saw them go in there, Captain," a voice pants. "His Royal Highness. And some servant girl."

Belle and Amir exchange frantic glances.

"They can't find me in here," Amir whispers. "My father'll know I'm sneaking out."

And Simone can't find out that Belle left. She's not losing freedom when she's so close.

There's a rough sound as someone shifts the grate.

"Here." Belle sparks with an idea. "Give me your cloak."

Amir doesn't even hesitate, pinning it around her shoulders.

"Get underneath it," Belle says, and the prince of

Miravale gets on his hands and knees in the muck and crawls beneath the cloak. "And keep your eyes closed, so the slippers won't work on you."

Things wouldn't end well if Amir emerged from the cloak, demanding to know who she was.

"You're sure you know what you're doing?" he whispers.

"You have to trust me," Belle whispers back.

There's muttering, footsteps, a torch's light looming around the bend.

Belle shoves her feet into the glass slippers. They're a little too big, but they'll do. They feel strange, too, nothing like glass; they're as soft and flexible as worn-in leather, as strong and durable as steel.

Just as Belle's yanked the cloak's hood over her head, several city guards and a rat-faced man burst into the tunnel.

They pause when they see Belle, and for a second her heart plummets into her stomach. She's gotten it wrong. They're not enchanted slippers at all, and Amir and Belle are about to be in big, big trouble.

But instead one of the guards scratches his head.

"Hello," the one wearing a captain's hat says. "We're looking for the prince of Miravale?"

"The prince of Miravale?" Belle repeats as gruffly as she can. "Took a wrong turn in the castle, perhaps, lads?"

"I'm *telling ya,*" the rat-faced man insists, and Belle scowls at him. "I *saw* him."

One of the guards humphs, and they continue down the sewer.

"Let's go," Amir whispers, but Belle shushes him. She doesn't want to risk anything.

Sure enough, the men return, clomping through the inch of water with disgusted faces like they're wading through a graveyard after a storm. Belle's pulse races, but she wills her face to be calm.

"Hello," the captain says. "We're looking for the prince of Miravale?"

They don't recognize her. The slippers work. She thrills.

"The prince of Miravale?" Belle's voice is so low, her throat itches. "Heard he's too scared of the dark to come down to a place like this."

Amir pokes her in the back of the calf.

The guard who had humphed jabs his baton at the rat-faced man.

"Last time we're listening to you, Ted," he grunts.

"Probably just wants some extra coin for the tavern," another sniffs.

"I'm *not lying,*" the man insists. "I saw the little prince himself. And some girl."

"Oh, hello there," the captain says, noticing Belle again. "Stay safe down here. Some questionable figures out at this hour." He shoots the rat-faced man a look of disdain.

When the footsteps recede, the voices disappear through the drain, and the grate clunks back into place,

Belle tugs off the slippers, and Amir wriggles out from under the cloak.

They look at each other and burst into quiet laughter, nerves and fear crackling into elation.

"I always get almost in trouble with you around." Amir smiles his gap-toothed smile. "I like it."

"Yeah," Belle says. For once, Belle is lost for words.

"Thank you." Amir rubs the back of his neck. "Belle, I . . ."

"Your cloak," she says, interrupting.

"Keep it," he says quickly. "I'm not cold."

"We should get out of here," Belle says. She places a glass slipper into each of her dress pockets, grateful for the cloak as the night air nips at them when they exit the sewer.

They hurry back in silence, more cautious this time, but Amir walks her farther than she expected, all the way to the end of the street before the Steinems' town house.

They stop near a streetlamp. Nearby a dog barks. Owls swoosh through the night.

"Belle." Amir's face is impossible to read.

"Thank you," Belle says. His tone is making her stomach flutter. "For the slippers. That was . . . Thank you."

"You don't need to thank me," he says softly.

They're standing very close.

Belle's palms sweat. Amir is looking at her like either she's sprouted a big hairy wart in the center of her forehead or he's about to free her from the manacle.

"It's a beautiful night for a stroll, isn't it?"

Simone's voice cuts through the dark. She's wearing a black silk nightgown and holding up a lantern, the light flickering strange shadows over her face. Belle might have been plunged into the ocean, so quickly do goose bumps leap over her skin.

"Go." Belle shoves a protesting Amir away as Simone ambles closer.

"Awfully elaborate plan," Simone observes, her gaze trailing Amir as he dashes down the street. "But you're nothing if not determined."

Simone knows about Amir. Belle feels sick.

"Follow me," Simone commands, and Belle has no choice but to obey as the manacle pinches her.

Her chest feels tight. She can't run; all she can do is trail Simone.

They descend into the cellar, Simone slamming the door behind them. The sound echoes, and Belle glances wildly at the window, like help might appear there, but beyond is just the garden, roseless.

Simone prowls toward Belle, her face distorted with fury.

"So," she hisses. "*Be honest.* You think you can outsmart me? Bend the rules?"

Belle has no choice but to nod, the manacle forcing her into truthfulness and her own dismay forcing her into speechlessness. She's just thankful the cloak hides the bulges of the slippers in her pockets.

Simone laughs, a laugh as cold as winter air and as unsettling as the fear in Belle's chest.

"Under no circumstances are you to leave this house." Simone's words are full of slamming doors, of all Belle's opportunities to escape that she didn't take fast enough. "And you are never to see, speak to, or be near Prince Amir again."

31

Ella

ANOTHER HOWL RIPS THROUGH THE woods.

Be brave, Ella commands herself, even though her heart beats so rapidly, it feels like she might choke on it.

The howling grows louder. Ella's blood chills. She can still hear the men from the village.

If they find the castle, Ella doubts they'll understand who Neesa is—they'll only see a beast. They could rally the other villagers, with their crossbows and pitchforks.

Another howl.

Ella races faster, and the woods help her in her mad dash. Branches swing open to let her through, falling into place to halt Maximus and his friends. Ella shivers as the growls grow so loud, she can nearly feel them, but she can't stop. Every so often, she catches glimpses of the castle's spires through the trees, relieved that it's close and horrified that Maximus will see it.

Silver shapes streak toward Ella, and she stumbles, crashing to the ground—the shapes flurry past her, leaving her unharmed. Their howls and yelps intensify as they get closer to the men.

Ella stays on her hands and knees for a moment, a new panic prickling through her. The cloak had swung as she'd fallen, smacking against a tree root.

The woods start to quiet. The men's yells and the wolves' yelps grow more distant as they're chased away. None of the wolves come back for her.

Ella reaches into her pocket . . . and stares at the broken glass, the butterfly dreams that are rapidly evaporating.

"No." She grabs fistfuls of air, knowing that it's useless as her eyes burn with bitter tears. "Please. No."

But the vial is broken. The dreams are gone.

Slowly, Ella pushes herself up and trudges toward the castle. No more wolves, no more villagers, and no one waiting to greet her. She wonders if they somehow already know that she's failed. It should have been such a simple task. How could she not have been capable of it?

She pushes the castle's door open. The main hall is quiet, and she follows distant voices to the library, where Neesa is lying on the couch and Stanley is stirring honey into her tea.

"Ella," Stanley gasps.

"You're here," Neesa says. Her ears press back. "I thought . . . You were gone for so long."

"I told you it might take a while at the alchemist," Stanley says quickly.

"You got it?" Neesa asks, and the hope in her beastly face cracks Ella's heart. What if they can't ever forgive her?

Ella can't meet their eyes.

"What's wrong?" Neesa asks. "Did something happen?"

"I don't . . . have it," Ella whispers. Her voice comes out rough.

"It's a rare ingredient," Stanley says, quick to soothe. "No surprise he didn't stock it."

"I mean." She clears her throat. "I got it. Um. I lost it, though."

"Lost it?" Neesa repeats.

"I was chased," Ella says.

"The wolves," Neesa realizes. "I forgot. They won't hurt you. They protect this place from people who hunt . . . beasts."

"Not wolves. Not exactly. Villagers. I fell, and it . . . it broke."

"Villagers chased you?" Neesa's voice is tight with anger, and Ella knows that this is all her fault.

"I'm so sorry," Ella mumbles.

"Get her something warm," Neesa urges Stanley.

"The warmest," Stanley agrees, scurrying away.

"I ruined it," Ella whispers. "The chance to break the curse."

Neesa makes a sound that, at first, Ella thinks is crying, only to realize that she's laughing.

"I'm worried about *you*," Neesa says.

"Me? But . . . Neesa. Your birthday is tomorrow."

Stanley returns with a platter of steaming pumpkin cakes slathered with butter and a saucer of hot chocolate.

"That means we still have a full day to break the curse," Neesa says, her words a little shaky. She touches Ella's face gently with her giant paw. "Are you hurt?"

Ella shakes her head. Her palms sting from when she fell, but nothing is broken.

One day. One day until Neesa is a beast forever. Until that village may be the last thing Ella sees outside of this castle. And in Miravale, Amir must be thrilled, anticipating the Revel.

"That's it." Ella reaches out and grabs Neesa's paw. Neesa flinches at first, as though unused to touch. "There's a contest at the Revel of Spectacles in Miravale. Whoever wins gets a royal favor. Neesa," Ella says, looking into her green eyes, "I could find a way to enter. And I could win. And the royal family could help you. They must be able to get us a fairy in time."

Neesa pulls her paw away from Ella.

"A king can't break a curse or force a fairy to do what he wants," she says. "Magic is stronger than a crown."

"But . . . but," Ella says, "surely it's better than nothing. And the king and queen of Miravale are kind. I've even—"

"No kings. No queens," Neesa interrupts. "I've already thought of that, and it won't work. Just drop it, Ella." She wipes her snout against the back of her arm. "I'm going to bed."

"Neesa . . . ," Ella begins, but Neesa's gone.

Frustrated, Ella paces back and forth, like she used to do in the cellar when she needed to think. It's terrible that Neesa's a beast. It's terrible that she can only explore Reverie through maps. But sulking about it isn't going to make it any *better.*

"You did what you could," Stanley says comfortingly.

Ella can't let it end like this. One day is nothing. One day is everything. If they can—

That's *it.*

She hurries to Neesa's room, bursting in.

"We don't need a festival," Ella announces. "Let's throw a party."

"A party . . . ," Neesa echoes. She is in bed, a book that looks impossibly small in her paws.

Ella knows how it sounds. It's not their best idea. But it's better than giving up.

"Fairies love a party," Ella says. "And I bet one will come—there has to be a fairy who wouldn't miss the chance to see a cursed beast in an enchanted castle. And then we'll make them change you back."

Ella glances toward the clock, although she doesn't need to look to know how close the hands will be to midnight.

There could be fairies at the Revel, but Neesa is right. It's too complicated. How could they get Neesa there?

"We can do better than a party." Neesa struggles to fight back a smile. "Let's throw a ball."

BY THE TIME ELLA MAKES IT BACK TO HER ROOM, it's nearly the next morning. She wants to plan the ball this instant, but tiredness hits her like a battering ram.

"Um. Hello." Stanley edges through the door as she's about to shut it. "I have something to ask you."

"What's wrong?" Ella nearly sways as she stands. Both her legs are unsteady from the sprint through the woods.

Stanley shakes his head and twists his tail around his paw.

"It's just . . . if the curse breaks, I'm afraid I'll go back to being nothing but felt. And I've so enjoyed being a real mouse." He sighs. "I love a nice Gruyère and a bit of port. I love the sunrise. I love being able to button and unbutton my vest." He buttons it to demonstrate. "How I love Gruyère. Can you imagine a life without cheese?"

"No," Ella agrees. "That would be horrible."

"Of course I want the curse to break," he says hurriedly. "But, you see, I just thought . . . I thought that perhaps when you catch the fairy, you might ask that I stay a real mouse."

Ella blinks. She hadn't considered that there could be downsides to a curse ending.

"Why are you asking me?"

"I don't want to make Miss Neesa sad," he admits. "This is the first time she's felt hope in a long while."

"We won't let you get turned back into a toy," Ella promises.

Stanley bows his head. Gratitude seems to embarrass him, which Ella understands.

"I shouldn't be telling you this," he says softly. "But, Miss Ella . . . things aren't what you think they are. There are certain secrets about this castle that . . . that may be worse than the curse."

"What secrets?" Ella demands, shocked into wakefulness, but Stanley has already slid out the door, taking his answers with him.

32

Belle

BELLE CAN'T SLEEP. SHE SITS ON THE BED, her legs curled into her chest, staring out the window.

She's tried, and her hands won't even move to open it.

Part of her hopes that Amir's face will appear behind the glass once again, though what good will that do now? She hopes for Henrik, the comfort of his hug, but then all this would be for nothing.

Tomorrow is the Revel of Spectacles. Tomorrow is the competition that was supposed to save Belle, Henrik, Villeneuve Trading.

It seems that Belle will have to listen to the distant celebrations through the cellar's walls. She'll have to hear about whoever Amir chooses as his champion from

Simone, Fiona, and Marie as she serves them dinner. And whenever Simone allows her to go back to Henrik, the ledgers will only fall deeper and deeper into the red.

At least Simone hadn't searched her cloak. The glass slippers are under the bed, behind a heap of dirty linens. Someday maybe they'll get back to Amir and his sister, or Ella.

The cellar door opens and closes. Marie enters, holding a candle. Belle's happiness at seeing her is tempered by the lengths Marie has gone to ignore her since the goblin attack.

"I heard you and Mama come back," Marie whispers.

The candle's flame is weak, and Belle can't see her expression.

"What do you think they meant? The goblins?" Marie trots closer. "When they said there was no beast of the woods?"

It's a question that's bothered Belle, too, a riddle that could be nothing or could be significant. But she's had other things to worry about.

"I just think it's strange," Marie muses. "That there's a missing princess. And those goblins said there wasn't a beast of the woods. Because I know there is. The mice say so."

"I'm sorry." Belle can't bear it. She's let them all down. And, really, goblins are unpredictable and tricky. They might know Reverie's darkest secrets, but the wickedest will do their best not to reveal them.

"Sorry?" Marie asks.

"About the goblins."

Marie drifts over to Belle's bed, sinking down beside her. Up close there's no anger in Marie's eyes, just determination. "That was the most exciting thing that's ever happened to me," she says.

"We almost died," Belle points out.

"Not almost. You brought the rooster before *almost.*" Marie glances at the door, back up to where her family is sleeping. "I was just . . . embarrassed."

"Why?" Belle asks. "You were so brave."

"You think I'm brave?" Marie repeats. "No one ever thinks I'm brave."

"All I did was throw a rooster," Belle says. "You nearly chased a goblin into the Dreamwood."

Marie watches a bit of wax drip down the side of the candle.

"What everyone thinks . . . They think I'm foolish. They think I'm dumb. But I notice things."

She stands, props the candle on a table, and unhooks the bracelet from Belle's arm.

"I notice things," she says softly.

The manacle of obedience lies motionless and innocent in Belle's lap, and her body prickles, like all her limbs had fallen asleep and blood's rushing back into them.

"Marie . . ." Belle gasps. She shoves the bracelet away, not wanting it to touch any part of her.

It's over. The manacle, after all this time, is off. She no longer has to obey. She can leave. She stares at Marie, a mixture of relief and gratitude and surprise swirling through her.

"I started wondering about that bracelet the goblin night," Marie says. "I thought it was weird. You didn't have it when you came." She glances at the door again. She's nervous, Belle can tell, to go against her mother like this. "I've been at the museums. And the library. I was trying to figure out why I recognized it. Your bracelet. It's a manacle of obedience, right?"

"That was really smart," Belle says, and Marie straightens.

"You think so?" Marie asks.

"I would be stuck here if it weren't for you," Belle says.

"Oh." Marie digs within the pockets of her skirt. "This is yours, too."

She holds out Belle's locket, with its gold chain and circular pendant dull from age. It could so easily be useless, a cheap thing.

Belle's heart feels squeezed in a fist. It's a kindness she wasn't expecting, and Marie has to take Belle's hand and pry open her fingers, place the locket in her palm. Its weight steadies her, like without it, she's unpinned from the earth. She clasps it around her neck, the magic warming her, like stepping into summer sunlight.

"I should have gotten it for you sooner," Marie says softly. "I just . . . I didn't . . . You showed me that I can do brave things."

The girls' eyes meet, and Belle is surprised by how one friend can remake the world. How sometimes you don't realize what you can do until you hear it from someone else.

The clock ticks loudly on the wall, and Belle springs into action. Soon the sun will rise, and Simone and Fiona will start ringing their bells, demanding scones with jam and honey, pigeon eggs freckled with parsley, creamy coffee, fresh-squeezed juice, a breakfast fit for a Revel morning.

"This whole time . . ." Marie's voice trembles. "You were just spending time with me because you had to, weren't you? You only saved my life with the goblins because you had to? Right?"

Belle digs through a pile of linens for the shirt and pants she came here in. She changes quickly and eagerly, clasping Amir's cloak around her. Dresses were fine and good if you liked that sort of thing, but they were entirely inconvenient for escaping.

As Marie's words sink in, Belle pauses.

"Of course not," she vows. "We're friends. I think . . . you might be one of my first real friends."

When she first got here, and she had to change Marie's sheets and clean sticky, half-eaten candy out of her dress pockets, she might have liked her a little less. But Marie and Amir are the friends Belle always yearned to have.

"Marie," Belle says. "Why don't you come with me?"

"Leave?" Marie's eyes roam the room. She swallows, her eyes falling to her feet. "I can't leave. Mother and Fiona are all I have."

Belle thinks she understands. Love runs deep, all ancient roots and tangled thorns.

"If you change your mind . . . ," Belle says, an open-ended promise. She rummages under the bed for the glass slippers and steps onto the mattress to clamber through the window.

"I'm sorry you got stuck here," Marie says. "But I'll miss you."

"I'll miss you, too." And Belle means it.

Then she's out the window, tugging the glass slippers onto one foot and then the other as she bolts through the gardens and out into Miravalc's streets.

When this is all over, when Belle's back with her father, she'll send a letter to Marie. She won't forget what her new friend did.

Belle only stops when she gets to the crowded market square. Even at an hour so late that it's early, the city crackles with life. And everywhere, there are purple banners and posters embossed with gold letters, announcing the Revel of Spectacles and the competition that night.

Belle grins, flexing her bare wrist. She has a contest to win.

33

Ella

FOR THE FIRST TIME ELLA LETS HERSELF CONsider what will happen if the curse doesn't break.

If Neesa stays a beast. If there's no returning to Elsweyr, no new beginnings, no adventures to distant lands.

Growing up, because of her leg, Ella wasn't able to take part in the games with the kids at the royal castle, the children of other scholars and advisers and armorers and diplomats. Even when her father brought home the glass leg, she didn't have the flexibility or strength to join in. Ella had to sit in the gardens, watching them shriek with laughter and tumble over the grass, and she had to endure the looks of pity and confusion from the other children. Even Amir hadn't fully understood. He was a prince. People shaped his activities around what he needed or felt.

And when her father got remarried, Ella held out hope for the bond of sisters, until Fiona picked on Ella for her glass leg or for having charcoal under her fingers, and Marie was often busy with harpsichord practice or playing with the neighborhood cats.

Here, for the first time, Ella feels like she belongs. Accepted for who she is. Tonight . . . if a fairy doesn't come or doesn't help them, Ella doesn't know what will happen to her. Will she be cursed, too? Unable to leave this castle for eternity? But here, with Neesa, it feels more like home than the townhouse has in years. Ella can't repay that by running to her own safety. Leaving Neesa alone. Forever.

She will stay. And they'll figure out forever together.

There's a small tap on the door, pulling Ella back to the present.

Tick-tick-ticking fills her head.

"Special delivery," Stanley says. The package he has is too big for him to carry, so he's pulling it along in his little toy train.

"What is it?"

"Your dress," Stanley says. "The ball is about to begin."

It's late. Too late. Just three hours to midnight. Three hours to forever.

But fairies prefer starlight, and so Ella and Neesa could do nothing but spend the day waiting, and planning, and wishing.

Ella lifts the dress out of the box, marveling at the

shimmer of the light blue silk. It looks like it could be made of rain.

"I don't need a dress," she protests. She's never seen something so beautiful. Light blue silk tumbles over a full skirt, with crystals stitched into the outlines of stars.

"Miss Neesa said you'd say that," Stanley retorts. "And she said you deserve to dress in something that will make Simone scream with envy."

Squirming with ribbons and ties that she really doesn't know what to do with, Ella manages to squeeze into the gown. It feels the way clouds might.

"Here. Let me help." Stanley motions that she should sit on the floor, and he leaps onto the bed. He takes the white rose she's kept behind her ear and starts to weave the petals into her hair, sticking in a few pins to make everything stay in place.

"What you said last night . . ." Ella runs her fingers along the crystal stars. Their conversation has been lingering in her mind. "What are the secrets?"

Stanley doesn't speak, just keeps tugging at her hair.

"Stanley!"

"This castle . . . It's not what you think it is," he mutters.

"What does that *mean*?" she asks. "Are we in danger?"

"There. Much better." He pats the top of her head. "Look. *You* could be a princess."

It takes Ella a second to realize her reflection is her. When she moves, so does the light, glancing off the dress. Her hair waves softly, white petals woven in like snow. Ella looks how she always thought she might look if she were a different kind of girl.

A strange feeling fizzes in her chest. She wishes her father were here to see her.

"What are you saying?" She ignores the feeling, glaring at Stanley. "What about the castle isn't what I think it is? Does Neesa know about this? You need to tell her, Stanley."

Nothing can interfere with the curse-breaking. What kind of secret is so terrible that Stanley feels the need to warn her but is too worried to say anything more?

"Forget I said anything." Stanley wrings his paws. "You're doing a good thing, Ella. A brave thing. Not just anyone would risk interfering in someone else's curse."

He ducks out of the room, only pausing to add, "If you wouldn't mind remembering what we talked about . . . I'd be ever so grateful."

"I couldn't forget," Ella promises. "When the curse breaks, you'll remain a real mouse."

What secrets could possibly be left? She and Neesa explored every inch of the castle.

Except.

As soon as Stanley is gone, Ella slinks down the hall as quietly as she can, pressing herself against walls whenever she thinks someone might be coming. She doesn't want them to know what she's thinking, lest she give false hope.

But Stanley and Neesa are making the final preparations in the front hall, and Citrine is probably still rehearsing how she'll greet the fairy, to calm her nerves.

Ella wonders: If you were a secret, where would you hide yourself?

There's only one place they hadn't visited.

Ella takes a roundabout route to the library to avoid anyone but ignores the library door.

A small spiral staircase swirls up behind it. Neesa had said that it was nothing. Was Neesa wrong? Was it something, like the fairy idea, that just needed fresh eyes?

The staircase is narrow, and Ella coughs as dust flurries up her nose and into her mouth with each step. It's not like Neesa has anything to hide. Ella's seen her worst secrets; they're written pretty clearly on her fur.

Finally, after Ella spirals up and up and up, she arrives in front of a curved door. Goose bumps prickle up her arms.

Giant scratch marks arch across the wood, like something huge and ferocious had attacked it. Only the claws of a beast could have done that. Past fury still seems to simmer in the air.

Ella had forgotten Neesa could be capable of that kind of anger.

She jiggles the door handle.

"Open," she command-whispers to the door.

It doesn't open, but this time Ella has help. She didn't spend the last few years living with Fiona and Simone and not learn a thing or two about picking locks. Unlike when she was trying to escape from the castle, Stanley has unknowingly armed her. Ella untangles a pin that Stanley put in her hair and edges it into the lock, feeling her way around.

The door swings open.

For a second Ella regrets coming up here. What if there's something in there that she doesn't want to see? What if there's nothing? She doesn't have time to waste on nothing.

But if there is something that could break the curse or affect the ball . . . she can't ignore it.

Cobwebs dangle, with bright-eyed spiders spying from the corners. It's dark. Soiled curtains are pulled tight over the windows, and dust has settled in thick layers.

Fresh air, Ella decides, is what this place needs. That's what fixed the other rooms in the castle. Maybe the secret to the curse is to make every last corner of this castle shine again, though she doubts that's true. But it never hurts to hope.

Ella yanks one of the curtains aside, but—it's not covering a window. It's covering a painting.

There's something about it. . . . It looks like . . . It can't be.

It's a painting of Amir. His eyes have the scrappy little spark that made her know that she would like him when she first saw him in the royal gardens.

But why would Neesa have a painting of Amir? Are

they in love? The thought is like a sharp-edged stone in her throat.

Ella feels a funny feeling, a little surge of jealousy. If Neesa loved him, why would she keep that secret? She thought that Neesa might— It was silly. A silly thought.

And beside it—one of Ella's maps of the Miravalian Palace. Why would Neesa keep this?

She tears the other curtains down, ripping them off to reveal more and more paintings in great wooden frames.

But they're not just paintings of Amir. There are paintings of the entire Miravalian royal family with—with the princess. The terrible princess who got Ella's father dismissed. Seeing her face makes Ella feel an anger she forgot she could feel, something raw and feral.

Ella stops in front of one. An autumn scene. Amir's face is alight with joking and daring. He dangles from the lower branches of an oak tree as his sister laughs down at him from a higher bough.

She can't figure out why Neesa has all these.

There's just something about these paintings that Ella—

It's the eyes.

Sparkling green eyes.

The same eyes that had laughed with Ella over breakfast this morning.

How?

No.

But.

It's *her.*

The wicked princess. Amir's sister. Anisa.

Neesa.

It feels like the castle has dissolved and Ella is tumbling down.

How had she not realized? They had never spoken. And everyone called her the princess, or Her Young Highness. Amir called her Ani. Ella called her nothing, out of spite.

But Neesa is—she's been kind. She's been funny.

Why hadn't Ella ever wondered, ever questioned? Neesa knew so much about Miravale. The castle only made Miravalian food. Ella *trusted* Neesa. They were *friends.*

But that doesn't change what she did. If it weren't for her, Redmond wouldn't have worked at the orphanage. If it weren't for her, Ella would still have a father.

"You're not supposed to be in here," a voice growls.

34

Belle

FREE OF SIMONE, WITH A HANDFUL OF HOURS before the Revel begins, Belle takes shelter in a public library, open all night, with large, comfortable cushions buried among the stacks. She awakens, stiff, as an elderly woman with tight wires of hair frowns down at her.

"Must have fallen asleep reading," Belle says, swallowing a yawn and skirting out of the library. She trips a little in the slightly-too-big glass slippers, but their magic is worth the inconvenience. Just in case, she's also pulled back her hair and tucked it beneath a cap, hoping she can pass as a boy. Easier to hide from Simone, and easier to avoid questions.

In the lead-up to the Revel, the city has been transformed.

Drifting among the morning crowds, Belle drinks in a pink city turned purple and gold from banners and decorations.

Purple flowers burst from every windowsill, from every buttonhole, from every hairdo. Vendors sell purple sourdough decorated with the royal family's crest as accordions bray and violins sing on street corners. Even the street urchins have gold ribbons wound across their chests as they snag purple pumpkin cakes when the bakers' heads are turned.

Across the street, glitter explodes from a cannon, and children squeal as they dash past, sparkles drifting over their skin.

The competition doesn't start until evening, and Belle spends most of the day in awe. It's one thing to hear the stories from her father, when Henrik and her mother came here for the wedding Revel. It's another to experience it for herself. After tonight their problems will be solved, including tracking Henrik down wherever he may have ended up.

Belle doesn't have any money, but there are enough free slices of buttered bread or free almond tartlets in the shape of crowns to fill her stomach, and plenty of entertainment to pass the day—acrobats and opera singers and a man who can burp bubbles in any shape you wish. Belle forces herself to focus on it all instead of thinking about what the evening will hold.

She rubs the locket so she doesn't get nervous. It feels

warmer than before, its gentle humming increasing like a cat purring, as though it knows something awaits.

As evening draws closer, Belle stands in a long line for free mushroom tarts. Lamps glimmer purple and gold, and a group of teenage girls trot past with lavender-flamed candles.

And Belle's stomach twists.

Across the street, in a wine-purple gown with a plunging neckline and an empire's worth of fake amethysts draping from her neck and ears and wrists, strides Simone. Fiona looks like a taffeta plum, and Marie is trailing them miserably.

Belle hurries away, pushing past people and not stopping to admire any of the stalls or attractions, even though she can hear the gasps and oohs and aahs of the crowd, the sizzle of roasting meat and the clang of a band and the rattle of some game. The slippers should keep her safe from Simone, but she's not taking any chances.

A woman with two pink poodles crosses in front of Belle, and as she tries to swerve around the dogs, one of the glass slippers gets caught on a loose cobblestone, falling off. Belle jerks back for it, but it's too late—a donkey, trotting past, steps on it.

The glass slipper shatters.

Belle winces.

A figure darts in front of her, catching her by the arms, and Belle cries out.

Amir pants, wiping a lock of hair out of his eyes. He's

wearing a velvet jacket with gold tassels and matching pants, but he still manages to look disheveled.

"Belle!" He stops her. "I've been looking for— Are you okay? Why are you dressed like a boy?"

"You were looking for me?" The slipper's enchantment must also be destroyed, which means that Simone will be able to recognize her, too.

Belle takes the other slipper off and tucks it into a pocket of her cloak. Bare feet it is.

"I went back to the cellar, but you were gone. I thought something might have . . ."

"It's a long story." Belle doesn't even know where to begin. But she knows she doesn't want to tell him about the manacle and the kiss. That's a story for another time. A long, long time from now. Then she notices his face. "Amir. Are you okay?"

He sniffs and swipes his sleeve over his nose. "Yeah. I'm . . . it's just . . . I thought my sister would be back before this. It's her birthday, too. It's supposed to be our Revel. But, Belle, why were you running?"

Belle feels sorry for him, but they can talk about his sister after this is over. Not now. "I have to enter the competition."

"The competition? Belle. You're . . . you're a kid. *We're* kids. It's too dangerous. They only let me watch."

Horns blare, and the crowds shift, people pulsing toward the center of the square.

Belle squares her shoulders. She's not letting anything else stand in her way.

"I have to," Belle says. "My family needs me to."

Amir's jaw tightens.

"You really need to enter it?" he asks.

"It's the most important thing in the world," she breathes. "Do you trust me?"

"Of course." Amir reaches behind Belle's ear, pulling the hood of her cloak over her ears. "Come with me. I'll get you in."

Amir directs her through a jostling crowd to an area marked by purple velvet ropes for the competitors. As people start to notice Amir, they cry out his name, and he peels away from Belle after whispering "Good luck."

Belle's with a group of about fifty people. Most are men or older boys, though there are two or three women. Belle keeps the hood tight about her throat. Even without the shoes, no one pays her much attention. There are foreign princesses to gawk at, rumors of a famous sorcerer in attendance, and, more importantly, discussions of the number of sword-fighting classes they'd taken in preparation for the competition, the number of push-ups they'd done.

Belle swallows.

She hadn't done any of that. But, she reminds herself, *they* probably hadn't fought goblins earlier that week. And surely, a royal competition required a little more than *push-ups.*

The rest of the crowd froths around the velvet ropes as

musicians play their violins, and a man wanders around, peddling greasy paper bags of sweet popped corn.

Belle's body is as tense as an arrow. She plays with the locket.

"Welcome, one, and welcome, all!" a royal attendant announces. "What a wondrous reason for us all to be gathering here today, in honor of our dear Prince Amir Perrault."

Amir is standing at the side of the stage, the queen beside him. Belle shrinks back, just in case the queen looks too carefully this way.

"We have so many delightful events in store for you," the messenger declares. "And this one needs no introduction. Throughout Miravale's fair history, every Revel of Spectacles has begun with a thrilling feat. But this one is even more extraordinary. These brave young men—"

"And women!" someone shouts from the crowd, and the royal messenger clears his throat.

"These brave . . . individuals . . . will compete in a hunt through the Dreamwood for one of its most dangerous inhabitants, and today's winner will receive a royal favor, granting them whatever they would like. Within reason," he adds hastily. "There are terms and conditions. We actually have them written out right here—" His voice is overridden and his pamphlets ignored as the crowd begins to buzz with anticipation.

Everyone except for Belle.

A hunt? Belle was expecting puzzles, performances of bravery and wit. Something that required speaking to spiders. Not a *hunt.* She's not going to hurt another living thing, and that's not what Miravale stands for. And . . . and she's not exactly sure how much good her locket will do on a *hunt.*

The trumpet booms.

The king's contest has begun.

35

Belle

THE CONTESTANTS ARE LED OUT OF MIRA-vale and to the meadows, steeped in nightfall. The Dreamwood beckons across the stone path.

There's so much chatter among the contestants, and so much shouting and laughing and giddiness from the crowd, that Belle can't hear anything clearly other than her heart pounding in her ears, each beat full of determination. People keep throwing glitter bombs into the air, sparkles raining down and sticking to Belle's cloak and hair. Torches blaze.

Belle squeezes the locket; it warms her hand. She'll win. She'll win. She'll win.

"There you go, there you go now, hurry up," a royal attendant says, shuffling people into line. Belle ends up behind a blond man thick with muscle who is proudly telling a short, wide man next to him that he eats four dozen eggs a day.

"Aren't you worried about cholesterol?" Belle chimes in.

"Cholesterol should be afraid of *me,*" the man says, barely looking at Belle before launching into another story. "Once I win, I'm going to have the prince appoint me to his royal guard," he declares, which Belle thinks is a little bit presumptuous. "You know the beast that lives in these woods? I saw a young maiden get *eaten* the other day."

"You did?" his friend asks, hanging on to his words eagerly.

"Almost," the man corrects. "She came through Kindlecrest and went into Dreamwood. I followed her to the beast's castle."

"Don't you mean cave, Maximus?" pipes up a red-haired man with the thick arms of a blacksmith.

"I laid eyes upon the castle myself," Maximus declares.

"Impossible," the red-haired man declares. "They say it's got magic hiding it, hasn't it?"

"Magic can't hide anything from me," the man scoffs. Belle grimaces.

"We saw it, too!" chorus the squat man and a twitchy man as lanky as a beanstalk.

"Did you save her? The girl?" asks a man with a long tangled beard.

The blond man flips his hair back. "She was half out of her mind," he says, ignoring the question. "Kept saying the beast liked pumpkin cakes."

Belle rolls her eyes. She's seen more bravery from a gopher, and more truth from one, too. But she's intrigued. The man's seen a castle? And Marie seemed so sure there was a beast, despite what the goblins said.

"But you didn't slay the beast, Maximus?" the other man confirms. "Or save the maiden?"

"I wasn't going to risk missing the Revel," the blond man huffs.

Belle has to cover her mouth to keep from snorting.

Soon Belle is led to a horse, and she ignores the attendant's offer of help in mounting it. Henrik had her on horses before she could even walk. Whatever they're being sent to hunt, Belle will outride all the men, find it, and bring it back to Amir, without harm.

Belle's prancing horse is surrounded by other prancing horses. Royal guards have to stand between the crowd and the contestants as people try to shove bits of cake and apples at the animals. She can't catch sight of Amir.

"On your saddles, you will all find a bow and some very special arrows—careful!" the royal announcer warns. Belle takes one out. Instead of an arrowhead, it has a soft, round tip with a metallic scent. Belle stuffs it back into her saddle, avoiding touching the tip. "They were dipped in a special sleeping enchantment. Because only that is enough to fell a magical creature and send it into eternal slumber, never to be woken again!"

There's an intake of breath, the thrill of anticipation, but Belle feels taut with nerves. She's waited for this moment for so long, and now that it's here, she misses the days spent wishing for it. That was much less frightening.

"Yes," the announcer declares. "The royal favor will go to the champion and hero who captures the goblin king! Who ends the plague that endangered our prince!"

Belle fills with dread.

Hats are thrown into the air. The contestants cheer and shout and whip their horses into action, and Belle throttles her horse's reins. An attendant walks around, offering torches to the contestants, but Belle ignores them.

"Justice for Prince Amir!" someone shouts, and the chant is taken up.

This is a terrible idea.

This might be one of the worst ideas Belle has ever heard.

Goblins live in strongholds, protected by nasty traps and trained in using nasty weapons. There wouldn't be anyone left to be champion. The lucky ones would be taken prisoner, and the unlucky ones . . . Well, Belle doesn't want to think about it.

She doubts her locket will do much good against goblins.

Far away, she sees Amir on a white stallion, flanked by attendants. But no matter how much she waves her arms, he doesn't turn to her.

She has to stop this.

So she turns to the blustery man next to her, who is busy studying his muscles.

"We can't go after a *goblin king,*" she hisses to him.

"What a strange little man you are." He tosses his mane of shining hair.

"Do you know how many goblins there'll be? At least a hundred. Not to mention the *traps.*" Belle's words trip over each other as she tries desperately to make him understand. "The spike pits, the trip wires, the weight-activated crossbows, the trained wolverines . . ."

The man has the good sense to look worried. The squat man next to him clears his throat.

"Maximus, maybe we'd better . . . I didn't sign up for spikes."

The rest of the entourage pale and mutter to themselves.

"Trip wires?"

"Wolverines?"

"You're right," Maximus blusters, looking relieved at a way out. "I wouldn't look nearly heroic enough standing next to some pathetic little goblin."

"That's not what I'm—"

"What we must do is something the world will never cease to talk about!" Maximus declares, flexing his arms like he's posing for his statue. Belle's heart sinks. This isn't at all where she was going. His face lights up with an idea as he announces: "We must capture the beast of the woods!"

"What?" Belle gasps. How he could think that's safer than tracking down a goblin king? Actually, Belle's not surprised a man like him would think that a brilliant solution.

"What?" the squat man next to him whimpers.

"Glory!" Maximus declares. "Fame! Your name in history!"

Belle tries to protest as his followers lean forward, their worry evaporating. Their excitement races among the other contestants, whose eyes brighten.

"Hopefully that maiden is still alive to be rescued. That'll be even better in the news," Maximus says to himself, and then he pounds his horse forward. *"Forget the goblin king!"* he roars, smashing his fist into the air. *"We go after the beast of the woods!"*

"No, that's not what the king . . . and the queen has forbidden—" the royal announcer blubbers, but he's no match for the golden-maned man. Even Amir blanches, but he's too far away, too many horses between them, to make his voice heard.

"Are you *mad*?" one of the female contestants cries out. "That's too dangerous!"

But Maximus's followers have infiltrated the crowd, and Belle catches whispers of fame, gold, renown throughout Miravale. Possibly even all of Reverie. Protests are drowned out by the rumblings of too many men who are staring, with a sense of awe, at Maximus.

"We'll rid these woods of evil once and for all!" Maximus waves his fist in the air. *"We capture the beast!"*

This is, somehow, an even worse idea. There is a reason Queen Milan forbade anyone to go after the beast before. It could be dangerous. And, more importantly, Belle is pretty sure that the stories of its terror are just that: stories. They could be hunting an innocent creature. But her voice and warnings go unheeded as more and more contestants take up the cheer.

"Capture the beast!"

36

Ella

NEESA TOWERS IN THE DOORWAY. SHE SEEMS much larger, much more frightening than Ella has ever known her, the candlelight glinting off those impossibly recognizable eyes and the sharp points of her tusks. She looks like she could shred all the paintings to pieces with one swipe of her paw, like she could rip out the oak tree that she and Amir once swung on.

"I told you," Neesa growls, prowling forward. "You're not supposed to be in here."

Ella's heart starts to clang with fear, but she holds her ground.

Louder than her fear is her fury.

"You lied to me," she says softly. It's something she learned from Simone. Keep your voice low in a fight.

Catch the other person off guard. "You said you were from far away."

"You can't be in here," Neesa says, but her voice has lost some of its power, like a paper cutout of a sword.

"You . . ." Ella's voice trembles. "You knew who I was."

"Ella—"

"*You* are the reason I'm here," Ella interrupts. "*You* were the reason my father had to leave the palace."

Neesa knows all about Ella, must have seen her countless times playing with Amir from her tower or on her way between lessons. And she knew Ella's father. She's heard how he died. She knows how rough the edges of Ella's life have been since. And through all that, she said nothing. Let Ella believe that they were really, truly friends.

"Ella," Neesa mutters. "Please. Let me explain."

"Just tell me," Ella says. "Tell me that you're *her*."

The princess of Miravale.

"I . . ." Neesa struggles. "I . . ."

It's all the confirmation Ella needs.

For a moment, Ella feels more beast than girl herself. In this moment she wishes she had claws so her pain could leave a mark.

"I hope you never break your curse," she hisses. "A beast like you deserves to be alone in the woods."

Ella rushes down the winding stairs and through the corridors, through the main hall decorated with glimmering ribbons and ice sculptures and floating candles for the ball, for a fairy that Ella won't be around to meet, realizing too late that she is barefoot and is wearing nothing but a gown stitched with stars.

"Miss Ella."

Stanley stands before the front doors, worrying the buttons on his vest. His face is crestfallen, his whiskers drooping.

"Please don't go," he says. He seems sadder than when he'd told Ella his fears about becoming a toy mouse again.

"Did you know?" Ella asks. "Who she was? What she's *done*? This whole time?"

Stanley's eyes widen, and he looks so regretful that Ella knows it's true. This was the secret. What he warned her of.

"Let her explain," Stanley pleads. "It's complicated, Ella."

Ella's lips curl.

"Curses aren't that complicated," she says. "All you have to do is *not* be someone who deserves one."

The door slams shut behind her, and Ella hurtles through the dark woods.

37

Belle

STOP THE HUNT!"

Belle's voice is drowned out. If hunting a goblin king had been thrilling enough, the thought of capturing the beast of the woods has stoked a fever. Men urge their horses into gallops, imagining themselves not just as champions. They'd be *heroes*.

"Stop the hunt!" Belle cries again, so loudly her throat aches.

Her horse pounds away from the other hunters and toward Amir. His stallion prances in place as Amir watches the hunt begin.

"Belle," Amir says, looking surprised.

"You have to stop the hunt," she gasps. "You can't send

those people to capture a beast. An eternal sleep? Amir. That's *cruel*."

"I'm trying," Amir says. "But, Belle, they're— *Look* at them."

Hunters ride so wildly that Belle is afraid they're going to start colliding with each other.

"That beast hasn't done anything to hurt anybody," Belle insists. "It's all just stories. You're sending them after an innocent creature!"

"Belle," he protests. "They won't listen to me! All they want is my father's favor!"

"Then *make* them listen!" Belle insists. "Isn't that what being a prince is all about?"

"It doesn't matter," Amir says. "They won't be able to find the beast's lair. It's hidden by magic."

"Unless you've already found it. And *that* man has." She jabs her finger toward Maximus vanishing among the trees, leading the pack.

"That's ridiculous," Amir whispers, blanching again. "He's lying."

"You can't risk that," she urges. "You want magic to live in harmony with Miravale? You're showing the Dreamwood you're its enemy!"

"Ridiculous," Amir repeats, looking horrified and lost.

Belle's brain itches. The man had said plenty of impossible things. That he eats four dozen eggs a day. That the beast likes pumpkin cakes.

Pumpkin cakes.

It couldn't be. . . .

Three years ago stories of a beast began. Princess Anisa disappeared three years ago, didn't she? With no word? But there had been so many pumpkin cakes ordered to the Dreamwood. And when she'd asked the goblin what had happened to the princess, it had said . . . Marie had even wondered . . . And no object would ever show the princess's location. . . .

A chill runs down Belle's spine, and she yanks at Amir's cloak, almost pulling him off his horse.

"Watch it— Belle? What are you *doing*?"

"It's Anisa," Belle whispers. "The beast. I think— I think your sister is the beast."

38

Ella

ELLA WANDERS, BLEARY-EYED FROM CRYing as she stumbles through the woods, the knee above her glass leg starting to ache again. She lost the path a while ago, but she doesn't care, and the rose petals had fallen out of her hair as she fled the castle.

The moonlight is a poor guide, but it wouldn't have mattered. Blinded by fury and betrayal, Ella has no idea where she's going, no idea where she wants to go.

The quiet of the woods is broken by distant shouts. It sounds like a group of men out on a hunt.

To avoid them, she veers among brambles, past shrubs, underneath branches, and when the pain in her leg is too great, she collapses in the roots of a great oak tree and starts to sob.

What will happen to her? She has no money. She has no family. The only people waiting for her are Simone and her stepsisters, and Amir. But Amir's *sister* did this, lied to Ella, over and over. . . .

There's the clamor of birds singing, and Ella glances up.

There are no birds, and there is no waterfall, though Ella can swear that she hears one, and the air starts to shimmer, the way it does after a storm.

A man appears beside her, and Ella leaps up, grabbing a stick to defend herself.

"Get back," Ella warns.

The man doesn't look like someone dressed for a hunt. His brilliantly blue waistcoat and matching nail polish are enough to startle every nearby creature. And Ella's sure that whatever he's using to perfectly slick his silver hair will only attract wasps.

The man grins. His teeth are as white as the roses surrounding Neesa's castle.

"That's no way to treat your fairy godfather," he announces, then pauses. "You *are* Ella, correct? Ella Aberdeen?"

"A fairy godfather?" Ella repeats. Maybe she's hit her head. "I don't have a fairy godfather."

Wouldn't the whole point of a fairy godfather be to *not* have to spend years doing your stepfamily's bidding? Or to not lose your father after never having a mother?

"But you do, dear child." The fairy is relentlessly cheery. Most fairies don't like sad things, Ella knows. That's why they give gifts to people they deem good, and curse those they deem bad, and then poof away so they don't have to see the consequences of either. "I go by many names, but recently I'm feeling particularly like Durchdenwald."

Ella feels like he should have chosen a name that's slightly easier to pronounce and remember.

"I've never heard of you," she says gruffly.

"I'm so sorry about your father," he says. "Redmond was a good man."

He knew her—

"You let him die," Ella spits, a yearslong fury spilling out. If anyone could have saved her father, it would have been a *fairy.*

"Magic can't undo death," Durchdenwald says sadly. "When I realized how sick your father was, it was too late."

Ella's lips quiver.

"I will *never* forgive you," she whispers.

"So be it. But hopefully you can forgive yourself."

"What?"

"Refusing to forgive can make us quite *beastly,* especially when we keep blaming ourselves." He clears his throat. "You have called me here now. What do you need? Is it your leg?"

He twists his fingers, and mist drifts in the air. The pain in Ella's knee evaporates. This seems like something he could have fixed sooner.

Ella doesn't think he deserves thanks. "Why are you here?" she says instead. "You've never come before."

Durchdenwald humphs. "I have other fairy godchildren. And a very active social calendar. I can't be everywhere all at once."

"I was living in a cellar." Ella glares at him.

"Oh." Durchdenwald taps the tips of his fingers together and wrinkles his nose. "Well. Challenges build character, et cetera, et cetera." He holds up a hand, looking uncomfortable. "Do not forget that I cast big magic for you."

"What are you talking about?" Ella is pretty sure that she's never experienced *big magic.*

"That." Durchdenwald gestures back toward Neesa's castle. "You thought that Princess Anisa Perrault was nothing more than a beast. You wanted her to feel the pain and loneliness you felt when Redmond died. It also happened that she wasn't so happy being a princess, so . . . lots of wishes to work with there."

Ella stares at him.

It can't—no.

But.

After her father's death, her grief had been so great, and the only way she knew how to handle it was to wrangle it into anger, wish curses and curses and curses to fall upon the princess.

Which means . . .

It's her fault.

She's the reason that Neesa is a beast. Those hateful thoughts she had after her father's death, a curse imagined and spun and cast. Her rage wilts.

"And when you wanted to hurt her *again,* who sent those birds to attack her, hmm?" Durchdenwald beams. "See? I listened."

"But . . . they attacked me, too," she gasps, barely able to breathe.

"Well, you confused them a little, didn't you?" he says. "Trying to rescue Anisa? They didn't expect that."

That bird attack in the garden . . . was because of her.

"And when you wanted adventure? *Hmm?* Seems like someone's been watching out for you."

"You . . . brought me here?"

"Yes. So maybe I knew about the cellar business," he confesses. "Maybe I felt a bit bad. And what's better than living in a castle? There may have been a bit of a mix-up, some annoying girl whose pirate magic interfered with mine, which was not my problem to fix, but *please.*" He claps his hands together. "Am I going to dwell on every little mistake? There's not time for that. And you got what you wanted, didn't you?"

"You mean . . ." Every breath feels like it's burning her.

"Yes," Durchdenwald says with a grin. "You are the one who wished for this."

39

Belle

THE WOODS PLUNGE INTO QUIET. THE shouts of the men, the clopping of horses' hooves, vanish into the air. There's some strange magic at play. It's too dark to see if a castle is ahead; Belle desperately hopes they'll never see it.

Belle and Amir exchange glances as their horses pound forward, racing after the men and their torches and bows. Amir continues yelling uselessly, the words snatched away as soon as they leave his mouth, but Belle doubts it would make a difference. Goblin fighting is one thing. Capturing a beast of legend, which would write men into the history books, has made them all nearly blind with the hunt.

They press their horses to go faster, faster, until they

reach the mob of contestants, torches burning and bows fished out of saddles. The hunters have paused.

Belle hopes it's because they have gotten turned around, twisted by the curse and going in circles.

But her hopes fail.

Through the trees, she sees a castle's spires.

Maximus wasn't lying. He has led them straight to the beast's castle. A beast who may be Amir's missing sister.

And then, a roar so great that it breaks through the magic, a collective howl from the men: *"Capture the beast!"*

40

Ella

"WHAT'S THAT SOUND?" DURCHDENWALD scrunches his nose. Elsewhere in the woods, people shout. "You humans like to make a lot of noise, don't you?"

"It's a hunt," Ella says dully, and then—

"Capture the beast!"

No.

Cold drips down Ella's spine.

No, no, no.

Neesa may be the bad princess, but—but—

She also showed Ella more than kindness. She showed Ella love. She gave Ella a place that felt like home. They laughed together, tried to catch fairies together, dreamed together.

And Ella wasn't any better than Neesa, was she? Neesa was a beast, but Ella was a Curse Weaver.

At least Ella has all she needs to save Neesa now: Durchdenwald. The original curse caster. She can end this, now.

"Break the curse!" Ella orders. "Break the curse so they won't hurt her!"

Durchdenwald shakes his head sadly. "I'm so sorry, my dear. But I cannot. I made the rules too specific. Only the false thief can."

"Me?"

"Smart girl." He beams. "And smart me. Quite tricky, isn't it? Only the wisher can save the cursed. And people say I could never be a poet."

"Then I have to get back to Neesa," she breathes. "Can you take me there?"

"You want to go *back*? There? After all this fuss?" Durchdenwald huffs. "Don't you want to wish for something a little . . . better? I've been practicing."

"She's in danger!" Ella urges. "Can you transport us?"

His forehead furrows like he's starting to notice Ella's urgency.

"Not with the curse," he says. "No fairy is able to enter the premises. I didn't want anyone messing with my work."

So the ball wouldn't have mattered at all. Ella's chest feels like it's full of seawater.

"I have to get to her," Ella says. Her heart gallops, booming in her ears. "Give me anything. Wings! Give me wings!"

He shakes his head again. "I can only transform a person with a curse, and I won't curse you, Ella dear."

"You're supposed to help me!" Ella exclaims. "But all you've done is make things *worse*!"

"There are a lot of mistakes with magic," Durchdenwald defends. "That's part of what makes it interesting. Like love."

He taps his finger against his chin.

"But that doesn't mean there isn't a solution. Maybe if we . . . I need something with an emotion attached to it. Do you have any particular fondness for any of these . . . leaves?"

He nudges some of the undergrowth aside, and Ella's eyes land on something large and orange.

"That." She points at the pumpkin. It reminds her of Neesa, of all the warm pumpkin cakes, the days before everything went wrong.

"A *gourd*?" He shrugs. "I never understand the youth. Well. It's your spell." Durchdenwald stretches his fingers and clears his throat. He chants, "Clickety-clackety, let this girl make a rackety."

"Is that really how magic works?" Ella asks.

He smirks. "No. I just like a little bit of drama. Now."

Smoke and glitter swirl around her. Ella coughs and bats her hand at the fog as the sound of clopping hooves fills the clearing.

A powerful horse prances before them, its flanks a

burnt shade of orange and its mane as green as a pumpkin vine. It lifts its long neck and neighs.

"Your steed," Durchdenwald says with a flourish.

Ella takes a step back, the terrible lurching feeling of flying through the air filling her body. "I can't ride that."

"Then you should have been a little more specific before I put all that energy into the spell." Durchdenwald pouts. "It takes time for magic to recharge. And I don't believe you have much time at all."

The sound of the hunt intensifies. In the distance, where Miravale must be, fireworks crackle in the night sky.

Ella swallows. If all that's standing between her and Neesa is a fear of horses, then she'll be brave.

"There's a lot we can learn from pumpkins," Durchdenwald says, giving her a hand up. "One seed can become many plants. Much like a single act of kindness."

Ella throws her glass leg over the horse, shaking a little at the massive beast beneath her.

"I'm sorry that your father is gone, Ella," Durchdenwald says. "It's easy to refuse to forgive. It's far harder to find that seed and plant it. Your father would be proud of you."

Ella's eyes burn with tears. And she remembers. "The toy mouse, Stanley. If the curse breaks, can you make sure he stays real? And Citrine? And the horses?" The tin soldiers?

A hint of a smile teases at Durchdenwald's lips. "I'll do my best." He slaps the horse's flank, and off it goes. "Now go do yours."

"Wait!" Ella twists around, realizing she's forgotten the most important part. "The curse! How do I break it?"

But Durchdenwald is gone, and the horse is moving too fast. Ella clings to its neck to avoid being tossed to the ground, her heart in her throat. She'll never get used to horses.

The air crackles with yelping and shouting; the men must have encountered the wolves. But a few wolves cannot hold off an entire pack of men.

The pumpkin horse moves swiftly and smoothly, and Ella's grateful to Durchdenwald for this, even though she can't forgive him for cursing Neesa instead of protecting her father.

Forgiveness.

Could it—

Refusing to forgive can make us quite . . . beastly.

That's the way to break the curse.

Or at least Ella hopes it is.

Because refusing to forgive makes you a type of thief. It doesn't steal anything, not really, but it still manages to leave you robbed.

The problem is, Ella isn't good at forgiving. She's never forgiven the king and queen for not doing more to save her father. She's never forgiven Simone or Fiona or even Marie for treating her so cruelly and making her clean the home that was once hers. Ella isn't sure she's forgiven herself for spending so much time wishing instead of doing.

The horse veers down a side path as the yips of wolves

ricochet through the Dreamwood, and the castle looms in front of them.

It looks dark, decaying, withered, worse than when she first saw it with Henrik. Snow has started to drift around it again, turning it black and white. Like Ella took all the brightness with her when she left.

The horse leaps over a fallen log, Ella gasping and clutching tightly to its neck and smelling a very pumpkin-y smell. The animal races through the Dreamwood and then halts like it's hit a wall.

Before the gates the mob waves bows and torches. The air is thick with smoke and their shouts.

"You best get out of here, miss." A man on a dappled pony leans toward her. "We're going to capture the beast. It might get ugly."

A hush falls over the crowd.

Ella hopes—she hopes and knows her hope is useless—that they've realized this is a bad idea. That they've all decided to go home.

But it's much, much worse than that.

Through the gates Neesa hulks in front of the castle, hunched and teeth bared. In the flickering torchlight, she looks every inch the fearsome beast. Her eyes glint green. She's all claws that could shred armor, all tusks that could crack swords.

Ella shouts at the top of her lungs, "She's a girl. The beast is a girl. She's *cursed.* You can't hurt her."

But the men either ignore her or give her funny looks. One tells her to read fewer novels.

"Neesa!" Ella shouts, but it's no good. The crowd's roar has built up again, this time louder and angrier than before.

Ella flings herself off the horse, the steed immediately tumbling back into a pumpkin. Ella shoves her way forward, through stomping horses and elbows pulled back to launch arrows.

"Neesa!" She bangs on the gates, crying to them. "You know me! I need to get to Neesa! Open!"

The gates listen, and Ella knows the risks. To get to Neesa, to save her, Ella must enter—giving the hunters access to the ground.

So Ella runs as fast as she can on her glass leg, horses surging about her and men shaking weapons in the air. Ella gathers all the fear, all the rage, all the love in her body and pummels it out into a fierce *"Neesa!"*

The crowd hardly notices, but Neesa does. She turns.

"Ella?"

The crowd closes in, shouting horrible things, a few men prematurely jabbing their bows in the air.

"I forgive you!" Ella cries.

Does she? Does she really? Part of her isn't sure. Part of her is still furious. Her father's death left scars. Neesa's lies still sting. But maybe Ella can be angry and still forgive her. You can feel two different things; you can be hurt and hopeful at the same time.

"I forgive you, Neesa!"

Ella can swear there's a glimmer in the air as she runs toward Neesa and doesn't let herself worry that she's just seeing what she wants to see. This has to be right. This has to solve Durchdenwald's riddle.

There. That is definitely a glimmer.

Neesa roars.

"I FORGIVE YOU!" Ella hollers. "ARE YOU LISTENING, DURCHDENWALD? *I FORGIVE HER.*"

The crowd seethes. Arrows are nocked, torches waving so wildly that sparks catch on the ground and flare.

But they don't flare as bright as the glimmer that blooms around Neesa and then vanishes with a pop.

The beast disappears with it.

And in the middle of the armed men, there's just a girl hardly older than Ella, standing and shivering in a ragged dress. Her hair is dark and tangled down her back. Her green eyes blink rapidly.

The crowd pauses.

It pauses, but not enough.

It starts to question, but not enough.

Someone hollers. A strangely shaped arrow zings through the air, its path smelling like metal. A horse whinnies.

The arrow falls to the grass before Neesa's feet.

And a green cloud blooms from the tip.

41

Belle

BELLE LEAPS OFF HER HORSE, AMIR CLOSE behind. They shove their way forward, past a large pumpkin and confused men and a girl wearing a ripped ball gown, a glass foot peeking out from the dirtied hem.

"Anisa!" Amir screams, and Belle sees her.

She's expecting a beast, but a girl stands among the men. Belle recognizes the similarities between Amir and his sister, the green eyes and bushy eyebrows, the long limbs, the nose with the slight bump.

Anisa trembles, wearing only rags. Her hair is tangled and drapes about her like a banner.

"Anisa!" Amir clasps Belle's hand so tightly that his touch could leave an imprint. His eyes are bright with

panic, his chest heaving as he rushes Belle with him through the crowd.

Anisa turns toward her, their eyes meeting, but something—something is wrong.

Anisa's eyes drift shut. Her mouth opens, like she's about to call Amir's name, but no sound comes out.

Belle sees the arrow shaft in the ground. The plume of green smoke, winding a sleeping enchantment around the princess.

And then Anisa falls.

42

Ella

"No!"

Ella rushes to Neesa's side, but already the princess's olive-toned skin—skin, not fur—is blanched and cold. Her eyelids flutter like she's in the middle of a bad dream. Ella pulls Anisa to her chest and feels for a pulse on the girl's wrist. It's there, but it's faint. Too faint.

Ella chokes on a sob.

"What have you done?" Ella cries out to the hunters. "You *monsters*."

The men fall quiet, a few horrified murmurs slipping between them. Slowly they turn their horses. Those on their feet back up. The air fills with the sound of bows clattering to the ground.

"Anisa! Ani!"

Amir, his eyes wild, lands on his knees beside Ella. Behind him is a girl with gray eyes and frizzy brown hair, wearing muddy traveling clothes and, inexplicably, no shoes.

"Get help." Ella's voice is hoarse from yelling. "Please, get help."

Amir nods, then sprints away, yelling orders. But the girl stays and stares at Neesa.

Neesa is so still, she looks like a painting of herself. Ella pushes a tangle of dark hair off her face, a face Ella had known and hated for years. But she doesn't hate her anymore.

"It's an enchanted sleep," the gray-eyed girl says quietly, like that *matters,* like Ella cares what's happening when all she wants is to *stop it* from happening, the way she couldn't stop her father from getting sick, couldn't stop his life from withering to a bed in a room with a window with a view of the world he wouldn't be part of again.

"Get *help*!" Ella orders, but the girl just stays there, clasping an old necklace like it will make everything better.

43

Belle

THE FIRST STORY BELLE HEARD ABOUT HER mother was that she once baked a pecan pie so delicious, it helped negotiate peace between two warring orc factions. She heard that her mother could solve a crossword in less than four minutes. Six, if it was in a different language.

What Belle heard about her mother was that she was the most extraordinary of women, a fact that Belle has clutched, like facts can morph into you and change your bones.

The locket is supposed to make her extraordinary. To help her win the competition that will change their lives. To make their business so successful, she'll stop feeling different. To make her father laugh like he used to, before the bad luck grew badder and badder. Her family's last hope, a final gift from her mother.

Staring at Anisa, the lost princess, the girl cursed to be a beast and then cursed into eternal sleep, Belle opens the locket. Passed down through countless years and generations—Belle's surprised to feel a tug, like this is what she was meant to do with it all along.

The girl in the blue ball gown stares at Belle like she's gone mad.

"What are you doing? Why aren't you *helping*?" she cries, her face and voice splotchy with tears and panic. "She's *hurt*."

Belle can't respond. Inside the locket is a tiny red rose petal.

That's it?

Belle lightly touches the tip of her finger to it. It's warm. A little silky. She'd been expecting something . . . more.

Maybe a dragon's tooth.

Or a phoenix feather.

Or pixie dust.

Just a rose petal. Her mother's favorite flower. This was the powerful magic Henrik spoke of? Belle had been hoping for something that seemed a little more . . . well, powerful. But despite how small and fragile it is, the petal gives off a warmth and hum far greater than it had when hidden within the locket.

Belle bends her head over Anisa, her hair brushing against Anisa's forehead. She can feel Anisa's too-weak breath against her cheek.

She thinks of her father and how much she wants to see him smile again. She thinks of her mother and how much she wishes she could hear Cora's advice. And she thinks of Amir, who believes Belle is someone worthy of glass slippers. There will be other competitions. It's worth risking the locket's magic to save this girl now.

And she places the rose petal on Anisa's chest.

Anisa's chest barely rises and barely falls. The locket trembles in Belle's hand, shattering into countless pieces, and Belle gasps, trying and failing to scoop up the shards. The other girl grips Belle's hand, points to where the petal is starting to melt, dissolving into a light pink mist that spreads over Anisa's body. It smells like summer mornings, like magic.

The girl in the ball gown's clasp is so tight that it hurts, their panic joined together.

The glow from the rose petal fades.

Anisa's chest rises and falls. Her eyelids flutter slightly but stay closed.

"Did it work?" the girl whispers.

They wait.

Aside from her chest rising and falling, Anisa looks as still as a painting. Belle's not sure if it was enough, if the sleeping enchantment is too powerful.

They stare at the fallen princess, their breaths catching, their hope so big, it's almost impossible to hold.

Then, slowly, Anisa begins to stir.

44

Ella

THE CROWD ERUPTS IN CHEERS AS AMIR AND Neesa—Anisa—step onto one of the palace's balconies. Behind them, Queen Milan and King Phillip look much older than Ella remembers.

Ella and Belle are tucked even farther behind them on the balcony, handed mugs of steaming cocoa and then promptly forgotten by the palace staff. Ella prefers this. In the chaos she would rather be invisible.

After all, this is her fault.

Though it is far past midnight, the Miravalian Palace is packed with people, and the sky overhead shines with stars and bursts with fireworks. News of Anisa's return has rippled through the city, drawing people out of bed, interrupting festivities. It's not every day a princess is confirmed to have been missing, and it's a very, very rare day that that princess is confirmed to have spent three years as a beast.

After Neesa had woken, Amir returned with a fleet of court healers and royal guards. They descended upon Neesa—Princess Anisa, Ella reminds herself *again*—and though she was a bit shaken, they declared her otherwise perfectly healthy.

Amir had secured two horses for Ella and the gray-eyed girl, but he was soon consumed by his mother, royal attendants, and court healers.

The girl was Belle, Henrik's daughter, Ella realized, just as Belle realized who she was: the person who was substituted into her life. There were so many questions, so many thoughts, that Ella's brain could barely manage to come up with a single sentence.

"I liked your maps," Belle said as their horses clopped along. She's talkative, telling Ella about the cellar, the rats, the manacle of obedience, the glass slippers.

Ella hadn't replied beyond a nod. The ride to Miravale had seemed endless and dreamlike. She felt like a made-up version of herself.

The past three years were all her fault.

By the time they arrived back in Miravale, the city was already launching a new kind of celebration, and Ella and Belle were dragged through the royal palace, asked a few questions by harried-looking secretaries and historians and the captain of the guard, before being ushered to seats behind the balcony for the royal family's announcement.

Now Amir and Anisa, whose rags have been replaced by a pale green gown and who looks so exhausted that Ella is impressed she's even upright, are a few feet away but somehow impossibly far.

Floating candles have been unearthed from storage and bob above the crowd.

The crowd mutters and gossips, and Queen Milan prods Amir forward. "They're waiting for you, son," Ella hears her whisper. Anisa glances back at Ella, but Ella can't meet her eyes.

"Good people of Miravale and our guests from throughout Reverie," Amir declares, and though his voice starts off shaky, it gains confidence. He's both the same boy Ella remembers and another boy entirely. It makes her sad and proud at the same time. "There are many rumors about what happened last night. But first I will announce the Revel contest's winner."

The crowd roars with delight. More fireworks explode into the sky, gold and silver shimmering above them. The man who had followed Ella into the Dreamwood steps forward, flashing a grin. Ella isn't sure why this matters anymore.

"My champion . . . ," Amir begins, and the crowd falls silent. It hushes, a collective inhale.

"My champion," Amir says, "is Belle Villeneuve."

45

Belle

FOR A MOMENT THE CROWD SEEMS AS SURprised as Belle is.

"Who's *Belle?*" Belle hears people murmur, but she doesn't care.

Someone hollers, "I knew you could do it, Belle!" And Belle spots Marie's red curls among the crowd. A guard guides Belle to Amir. Her heart is hammering. She did it. *She did it.*

"The Revel of Spectacles was unusual this year," Amir announces. Belle's surprised by how . . . *princely* he seems. "Belle didn't win. No one won. But Belle did something much better. She saved my sister."

He beckons at Anisa, who waves weakly. From the hunt to now, the royal staff has been fussing with her, combing her hair and braiding it so it falls down her back, but she can barely keep her eyes open.

"My daughter. Oh, my darling daughter!"

Henrik surges onto the balcony from inside the palace, two guards looking frazzled as they try to keep up with him. Belle doesn't know how he managed to get in, but she learned to stop questioning Henrik years ago. His patched traveling coat flies behind him, his face is slightly sunburned, and there are twigs in his hair.

He clasps Belle tightly, and she's swept with a tide of relief and delight.

"Belle! You wouldn't believe the things I faced to find you—there was the castle in the Dreamwood, of course, but that's a later story, and then the Huntsmen, and then a wrong turn led me to a swamp full of cockatrices, if you can imagine." Belle could, in fact, believe it. Henrik always manages to find trouble. She's sure that Ella's ending up at Anisa's castle had something to do with that. "But what you've done . . ." He sweeps Belle up into a hug. "Your mama would be proud."

"It was the locket," Belle mutters, thinking about the cellar, the manacle, all the not-so-great things that happened.

Her father shakes his head and pulls her back into an embrace. "It was *you,*" he says. "The magic may have been able to break the princess's enchantment, but you chose to use it. You . . . I know what that locket meant to you, my Belle."

"It's true." Amir steps forward. His cheeks are flushed, whether from excitement or nerves, Belle can't tell. "You figured things out. Over and over. You . . . I don't know what would have happened to Anisa if you weren't there."

The words warm Belle, though she didn't even realize she was cold.

"Sorry. I don't mean to interrupt," Amir says hurriedly.

"Your Highness." Henrik bows his head, stepping out of the way. Amir protests at the title but, at Henrik's insistence, approaches Belle. He extends his hand. Belle stares in shock.

It's her locket. It's crisscrossed with the hairlines of cracks, but it's whole.

"I think the magic is gone," Amir says softly, pressing it into Belle's hand. "But I thought you might still want it."

"Thank you," Belle whispers, her voice hitching. Amir takes her hand, tugging her to the front of the balcony. It's almost dizzying how many people are looking up at them, some standing on top of fountains, others climbing trees or trying to clamber onto lower balconies.

"As the prince of Miravale, it's my honor to offer a favor to you, Belle Villeneuve, on behalf of the royal family," Amir says. He glances behind him at the queen, who nods. The words sound rehearsed, but his smile and enthusiasm are genuine. "What can we grant you?"

The crowd once again begins murmuring, different languages swapping their yearnings.

"A villa."

"A king's fortune."

"Ageless beauty."

"A pet ostrich!"

Already Belle can feel the rattle of carriage wheels under her, the smell of roasted coffee mingling with pine needles during their mornings on the road. The sensations of Villeneuve Trading.

"My father's merchant business restored." She clears her throat to speak louder and glances back at Henrik, who's beaming. "The best and fastest ships that your ship-makers can build, and some of the top sailors Miravale can spare. And a new caravan."

Amir still hasn't dropped Belle's hand. His is getting a little sweaty, but she hopes he doesn't let go. At first Amir was a prince to kiss to win her freedom, but now he's something . . . more.

"Of course," he says. "All of it. Granted. I mean, I think I can say that." He glances behind at the king, who dips his head in a nod. "Yes. Granted."

Behind them Anisa gasps. The queen hurries to her side.

"What's wrong, darling? Are you all right?" She presses the back of her hand to Anisa's forehead, but Anisa shakes her off.

Even below, the crowd can sense that something is amiss.

Anisa stares over Belle's shoulder.

"Ella's gone," she whispers.

46

Ella

CLUTCHING THE FOLDS OF HER BALL GOWN, now coated with mud and smelling like pumpkin, Ella rushes through the Miravalian Palace. She knows it well enough, all those days spent wandering it with Redmond and bringing it to life through her maps. Days when she had hated Anisa, imagined terrible fates for her, until she became beastly herself.

Though there are gaps in what she's seen of the palace, Ella knows which stairs wind down the fastest, which hallways veer toward the courtyard, which doors spill out into escape routes. It's quiet now, the royal family and the public concentrated at the back. No one is here. No one is looking for a scullery maid.

Ella refuses to wake up tomorrow in a cellar as little

bells ring, demanding breakfast. But what other options are there for her once the royal family figures out that she was the one to curse Anisa?

At least Durchdenwald gave her this: the knee above her glass leg doesn't ache as she runs through the corridors and into the Everlasting Garden. The night air is brisk and sharp against Ella's bare arms, and she presses herself against the walls whenever a guard passes. She wishes she had those glass slippers Amir always talked about.

Finally, she winds her way to the queen's rose garden, where the rosebushes are tame and elegant. Ella slows, catching her breath, trying to reason out a plan. She's good at in-the-moment decisions, but planning ahead is harder. There's the matter of money for a carriage or an inn, and the matter of being only twelve, and the matter of Simone sending the guards to look for her. . . .

"You're not supposed to be here."

Ella freezes.

Anisa stands at the entrance to the rose garden, a few pieces of hair escaping from her braid. Her green dress swishes in a breeze. She looks worried. And strange. And familiar.

"Everyone's waiting for you," Ella says weakly.

"I don't care about them," she says. "Where are you going, Ella?"

Her voice is different. And strange. And familiar.

"Are you leaving?" Anisa's words tremble slightly. "It's not because of me, right, Ella?"

Ella grimaces. It's the only thing her mouth feels capable of. She doesn't want to say anything, but it would be worse to wonder when Anisa will find out on her own.

"I caused the curse," she whispers. "I'm so sorry. It's all my fault. I—a fairy—it's my fault. It's better if I just go."

Anisa rushes toward her, and Ella braces herself. But instead of fury, she's met with a hug, Anisa pulling her deep into an embrace, her hair tickling Ella's nose.

"There wouldn't have been a curse to cause without me. I have a lot to apologize for, too," she says. "And, Ella, you're the one who broke it. You risked so much to do that. Please. Don't go."

Ella bites her lip. She hadn't realized how much she wanted to hear those words. She hugs Anisa back. Durchdenwald was right again. Perhaps she needed to be forgiven just as badly as Anisa did.

"I saw you run away, Cinderella. Didn't want to say hello to your darling stepmother?"

Simone stalks forward. Her dark dress sweeps around in a tide of velvet, and her pale skin nearly gleams in the moonlight.

Ella flinches, and Anisa takes her hand. She felt so emboldened, so ready to face Simone when she was in Neesa's palace, but here she feels like she's eight again, promising her father that she'll be a good stepdaughter, that she'll help build a good family.

"Your Highness, I'm so sorry for the inconvenience my stepdaughter may have caused."

"Inconvenience?" Anisa's voice rises. The curse may have broken, but it seems her temper hasn't.

"Did everyone neglect to realize that the celebration was on the *other* side of the palace?" The queen, followed closely by King Phillip, Amir, Belle, and Henrik, paces into the garden. "Anisa, my love, what are you— Oh. Lady Simone."

"I've just come to collect my stepdaughter, Your Majesty," Simone declares. "I hope she hasn't been too much of a burden."

"Burden?" Queen Milan strides forward, placing her hand on Ella's shoulder. Simone stares at it, blanching with shock. "Your stepdaughter helped break a curse. In three years she's been the only one to find and befriend Anisa. She brought my daughter back to me."

Simone's lips curl, but suddenly Ella doesn't care what her stepmother has to say. She *did* break a curse. She *did* befriend a princess trapped as a beast. She confronted a *fairy.* She rode a *horse* made out of a *pumpkin.*

Ella steps closer and whispers so that only Simone can hear. Simone smells like a bouquet of flowers about to rot.

"Why?" Ella mutters. "Why do I matter so much to you?"

Simone's nostrils flare with a look like if she could breathe fire, Ella would have to dodge the flames. "Because your father left you to me," Simone says, looking surprised at her own honesty. "It's my job to make you *good.*"

"You?" Ella's frustration feels thunderous. "How could *you* ever teach me what it means to be good? You trapped Belle with that bracelet! You made me sleep in a cellar!"

"You ungrateful little . . . ," Simone splutters. "I have not—I would never—how dare—"

"All I wanted was for you to love me," Ella whispers, surprising herself, too. That's why she'd always listened, even when it meant she was sweeping cinders. Because she *hoped.*

Simone looks like she's been slapped. Her jaw grinds, and her eyes glimmer, and Ella realizes how long she hoped for a happy ending in that house, with her stepfamily. But sometimes our stories change. What our happy endings look like do, too.

"You can't have her!" Anisa declares, and Simone draws back into the shadows, worry flaring in her eyes. "She's a brilliant mapmaker, and you locked her in her own cellar and made her wash your dirty laundry!"

Henrik clears his throat, stepping forward.

"Perhaps I can offer a solution," Henrik suggests. "One that is a bit selfish. It's rare to encounter such a curious mind, a fearless spirit, and, I have overheard, a talent for mapmaking. I would like to invite you to join our little troop."

Ella stares at Henrik. Belle nods in encouragement. She's still a stranger, but Ella feels like they know each other deeply.

"Join you?" Ella murmurs. All this fuss . . . for *her.* She dreamed so long of opportunities, of impossibilities. But Ella has learned that there isn't such a thing as impossible.

"Belle and me," Henrik says. "There'll be room in the new caravan."

It's . . .

He's offering her an adventure. A proper one. An endless one. And, maybe, an unconventional type of family.

Simone's face is twisted like she's in pain. "Go," Simone spits, so quietly that only Ella can hear her. "You're more trouble than you're worth. And . . ." She pauses, her expression unreadable. Her voice drops. "This is the kind of life your father hoped you would have."

In Neesa's version of the story, she was the trapped princess, not an evil one. Maybe in Simone's version of her story, she's the stepmother doing what it takes to survive, not the wicked one.

As Simone strides out of the garden, only Queen Milan and Ella watch her go.

"Going with Henrik . . . That's everything you wished for," Anisa says softly. She tries to sound happy, but she looks suddenly wilted, like a flower left without water.

Anisa spoke of seeing Reverie, of wandering with a map instead of staring at one in a library. And here she is, at risk of being trapped once again. The curse may be broken. But broken curses aren't always enough for happy endings.

"Only if Anisa can come with us," Ella says, adding quickly, "if she wants."

The queen and king stiffen. Anisa's eyes widen. Ella's palms prickle.

"Excuse me?" King Phillip asks.

"Give them a minute, Phillip," Queen Milan interrupts.

"I don't see why not," Henrik says slowly. "As long as that's not considered kidnapping a princess? We'll have enough to worry about without arrest warrants."

Anisa gave Ella hope and friendship and a home. She deserves to see the world, to be part of it.

"If you want," Ella repeats quickly.

"I want to go," Anisa says softly, her voice a little wobbly. "Of course I want to go."

The queen blinks rapidly, folding her arms over her chest like the words have wounded her.

"I can't forgive myself for all the years we spent apart. For not being with you, no matter what," the queen says. "I thought—I thought you being in the forest castle, with your things . . . And we had the court scholars working on the riddle, but . . . but I . . ." She clasps her hands tightly, like there are things too painful to say. "Perhaps we all should have worked harder to learn from the curse, rather than hiding from it."

The king clears his throat. "Perhaps if we hadn't tried so hard to protect you, none of this would have happened," he admits.

Queen Milan takes Anisa's face in her hands. "I will miss you," she says. "But it's far more important to know that you will be happy."

Ella's dreams were never wild enough to believe something like this could come true, but maybe that's the point. Maybe sometimes we don't recognize our dreams until we take a wrong turn into them.

47

Belle & Ella

A WEEK HAS PASSED SINCE ANISA'S RES-cue, and now Belle, Ella, Anisa, Henrik, Citrine, Stanley, and Amir gather around the Villeneuves' new caravan at the edge of the Dreamwood. Sunlight drips over the road leading into the woods, and Miravale's pink walls blush behind them.

Most of their goodbyes have already been said.

Belle taps the side of the caravan. It's much nicer and larger than the lopsided one she and her father had be-fore, this one enchanted to move without needing steeds. Painted as blue as the sky, there's plenty of room for trea-sures untold, three girls, one merchant, and a toy mouse who is very much real and has made sure the stores are well stocked with Camembert and lavender sheep's-milk cheese.

Stanley was fetched from the Dreamwood the day after Anisa's rescue, still felt and still able to enjoy Gruyère. Over the past week he's thanked Ella by bringing her so many pumpkin cakes that she's starting to wonder if she'll turn into one.

Citrine soars overhead, sunlight glancing off her jeweled wings as she bids them goodbye. She was adamant about staying at the Miravalian Palace to gossip with courtiers.

Amir loads a telescope into the caravan and comes to stand beside Belle.

"You're sure you're not coming?" Belle immediately wants to swallow the question. He's made it clear that he's not leaving, determined to help his father learn how to peacefully solve the goblin problem. They are, he emphasizes, just misunderstood.

All week Belle wished that his mind might change. She sprinkled conversations with the delights that they'll encounter: fields of talking flowers, staircases made of sunbeams, witch communes, and rumored giant kingdoms in the clouds.

"Are you sure you're not staying?" Amir counters, like he's hoping that she'll change her mind, too. Amir has assured her she can live in the castle in Henrik's absence, enjoying royal tutors, performances by fire swallowers, the finest food in the city, unicorn riding lessons. (Sure, he'd have to catch one, but he promises he'd do it for her.)

"Not yet," Belle says.

Amir takes her hand, turning a little pink. "I'll wait," he says.

"I'll write," she promises.

He bends down, catching her fingers in his, and kisses her hand. Belle flushes. It's much, much better this way, she decides, than when she was trying to use him to get free of a bracelet.

Ella watches them from afar as she double-checks that there's a box of charcoal and a supply of fresh paper in the caravan. There will be many maps to make in the coming months.

"Belle doesn't seem to think Amir's a frog." Anisa's green eyes latch on to Ella's, growing thoughtful. "Ella . . . I'm starting to wonder if this is what I wished for all along."

"Me too," Ella admits. But it's kind of fun, discovering who else you could become, what other wishes you may have. "What do you think it'll be like out there?"

"I don't know. But I promise not to get us all cursed," Anisa says. She takes Ella's hand, and Ella can't help grinning.

"Don't promise to be *boring*," Ella replies.

"Come on, then!" Henrik waves out of the caravan. "Adventure isn't going to find itself."

And they found their way into exactly the right story.

Acknowledgments

I grew up telling and retelling myself variations of "Cinderella" and "Beauty and the Beast," the Harry Potter tales (thankfully, the Harry Potter fan fiction got lost on old computers), the Lord of the Rings trilogy, the Chronicles of Narnia . . . The list continues.

After all, that's part of the magic of stories, and fairy tales in particular: they can be told over and over, every version true, and they make our world bigger as we imagine them through our life and lens.

Getting to retell stories I love in this book was a rare kind of joy, thanks in large part to so many fabulous people.

Thank you to everyone at Random House Children's Books, with heaps of extra love for my editor, Tricia Lin. I'm a big believer in everyday magic, but there was something truly special about meeting you and creating Reverie. You always knew where the story needed to grow and where it needed to pause, and I feel ridiculously lucky to have your thoughtful eye, kind words, and shared *Dragon Age* fandom in my corner. Thanks also to Caroline Abbey, Mallory Loehr, Michelle Cunningham, Michelle Crowe, Rebecca Vitkus, Barbara Bakowski, and Tracy Heydweiller.

So much appreciation for the crew at KT Literary, especially Hilary Harwell. You are a stalwart champion of my stories and an answerer-of-random-questions. I can't wait for all the adventures to come.

Thank you to everyone at Georgetown University and the University of Arizona MFA program who supported, nurtured, and made my work much, much better. In particular, Manuel Muñoz, who guided me through a thesis where I secretly wrote a fantasy novel on the side. Thank you for reminding me there's a place for magic in all my stories.

To all my fellow MFAers, retreat and conference buddies, mentors, writer friends, and book nerds—there are too many to list, but you know who you are, and I treasure the community we've built.

It would be out of character not to thank Stephen Schwartz and Gregory Maguire for *Wicked* and Andrew Lloyd Webber for *The Phantom of the Opera,* stories that continue to stoke my obsession with antiheroes.

To my family: Mom, Dad, Jen (I'm so lucky to also call you my mother), and Tyler (the best little brother anyone could ask for). All the library trips, movie nights, Barnes & Noble runs, *Halo* games, and summers in the San Juans helped shape me as a storyteller. I love you all very much. And, Dad, you told me when I published a novel, you'd get me a dog. I'm ready to collect.

To Brookie: I have to include you, or you'd never let me forget it. You're my favorite sister.

To Aidan, for always knowing when I need a sweet potato or a sunset and for believing in me even on the days I don't believe in myself. You make it much easier to write happy endings. And, of course, to Banks and Fromage.

Most importantly, to my readers: Wow. I feel incredibly grateful that you're holding this book in your hands. Now go befriend some beasts and break some curses—I can't wait to hear your fairy tales.

Your Royal Highness,

you requested another Princess Swap?

Your wish is our command. . . .

Read on for a peek at the story of Snow White and Sleeping Beauty!

Once upon a time, a princess's heart turned to stone.

No, sorry. We're not there yet.

Let's start over.

Once upon a time, two princesses betrayed each other for a crown—

No. Now we're starting too early.

But pay attention. Fortune favors those who can see things for what they really are.

We'll begin here instead:

Once upon a time, there was a queen who went hunting for a curse.

She came from a long line of queens who had a history of untangling, breaking, and, on rare occasions, casting curses.

But the history books will tell you that she found herself pregnant with no curse necessary. After all, there are certain things you want to keep away from history's eyes.

The impending princess's birth was a cause for celebration. A single princess was always born in this kingdom, to one day take over the throne, and it had been that way for centuries upon centuries, and centuries before that.

Of course, no other queen needed to resort to curses in order to have a child. No other queen had tried, year after year, to conceive a child, only to watch the royal nursery remain empty.

Before the princess's arrival, the kingdom's people gossiped about the color of her hair: Would it be black, like her mother's and like the kingdom's First Queen's? Or half copper, half gold, as a queen's was every century or so, the same as the First Queen's wicked sister's?

While they picked up their bread at the baker's, they debated what the princess's birth might mean for their taxes.

At the pub at night, they wondered what fairy blessings the new princess might receive.

In this kingdom, magic always lurked close at hand. It sprouted from the soil and would stain your fingertips, and you were at risk of being zapped into a ferret if you were a little rude to a touchy banshee. And for each of Apfel's princesses, seven of Reverie's good fairies bestowed a blessing upon the child.

Perhaps you can see where this is going.

But no one else did. Instead, the entire kingdom of Apfel rejoiced. With every birth came plentiful crops and unexpected treaties between warring goblins or angry bandits. Gold coins would appear in the gutters, within loaves of bread, in the heels of shoes.

Except before *this* princess was born, gold coins crumbled into dust. Dirt roads turned to mud, even on sunny days. Pigeons refused to deliver mail. Milk curdled in pails, bread hardened to iron, and pillows vanished from beneath people's heads halfway through the night.

Taken alone, these could each mean plenty of things.

But few saw how the queen's belly grew larger and larger as she fell sicker and sicker, how the paintings of the past queens lost their smiles. In the castle's courtyard, two apple trees bloomed year-round, one with red blossoms and the other with flowers as pearly as snow. But now none appeared on the branches, and all the leaves fell to the ground.

The king and queen worked to ensure no one thought *curse*. The queen had not meant for this to happen. She didn't realize what she had offered to give up.

So the royal family ordered gold platters for the feast, and the chefs worked without sleep for three days. Artists calligraphed the invitations. Outside, storms began.

You know what comes next, don't you?